7

ScottForesman

Accelerating English Language Learning

Authors

Anna Uhl Chamot

Jim Cummins

Carolyn Kessler

J. Michael O'Malley

Lily Wong Fillmore

Consultant

George González

ScottForesman

Editorial Offices: Glenview, Illinois

Regional Offices: Sunnyvale, California • Atlanta, Georgia

Glenview, Illinois • Oakland, New Jersey • Dallas, Texas

ACKNOWLEDGMENTS

Illustrations Unless otherwise acknowledged, all illustrations are the property of Scott, Foresman and Company. Page abbreviations are as follows: (T) top, (B) bottom, (L) left, (R) right, (C) center.

Louise Baker 10–11; Deborah Wolfe/Skip Baker 34–35; Shawn Banner 87(B), 164–175; Melissa Turk/Ka Botzis 218(T); Edward Burton 114, 192–193(B); Deborah Wolfe/Anthony Cericola 219(R), 224(L); American Artists/Lane Dupont 122(B), 214, 216–217(BC); Cecile Duray-Bito 42(C,B), 43(C), 45(T); Howard S. Friedman 184–185; Steven Edsey/Mike Hagel 2(B), 24; Christina Tugeau/Laurie Harden 123(B); American Artists/Doug Henry 102(T), 104(T); Melissa Turk/Susan Johnston-Carlson 6–7, 8–9; Dilys Evans/Laura Kelly 119, 187; George Kelvin 57(T), 61(B); Bob Lange 32(T), 33(BR), 78(T), 79(R), 83(T), 85(B), 100(R), 107(T), 170(T); Carol Chislovsky/David Lund 88–89, 110(T); The Schuna Group/Cathy Lundeen 48–49; Mapping Specialists 106, 109(T), 156, 194–195; Carol Chislovsky/Paul Mirocha 182–183, 190; Square Moon/Elizabeth Morales 198(C), 222–223(B); Pamela Paulsrud 142–143; Deborah Wolfe/Saul Rosenbaum 222(T); Raymond E. Smith 188(TR); Melissa Turk/Wendy Smith-Griswold 50–51; Christina Tugeau/Frank Sofo 197(B), 228; Gwen Walters/Susan Spellman 44, 46–47, 58–59(B); Richard Salzman/Wayne Anthony Still 76, 84(T), 86(T), 87(C); Darren Thompson 226–227; Carol Chislovsky/Cathy Trachok 60(B), 176; Christina Tugeau/Meryl Treatner 109(B); Randi Fiat/Tracy Turner 202–213; Elaine Wadsworth 200(T)–201(T); Vicki Wehrman 52; Elizabeth Wolf 38.

Literature 12–23: HOW MANY DAYS TO AMERICA? by Eve Bunting. Text copyright © 1988 by Eve Bunting. Illustrations copyright © 1988 by Beth Peck. Reprinted by permission of Clarion Books/Houghton Mifflin Co. All rights reserved. 64–75: THE RIVER THAT GAVE GIFTS by Margo Humphrey. Copyright © 1986. Used by permission. 88–99: From KNIGHTS OF THE ROUND TABLE by Gwen Gross. Copyright © 1985 by Random House, Inc. Reprinted by permission of the publisher. 112–113: Excerpt from the Travels of Marco Polo translated by Janet Battiste. 126–137: HEY AL by Arthur Yorinks. Illustrations by Richard Egielski. copyright© 1986. used by permission. 164–175: "The Nazcas' Secret" by Carol Anderson in HIGHLIGHTS, November 1993. Copyright © 1993 by Highlights for Children, Inc., Columbus, Ohio. Reprinted by permission. 202–213: "Jealous Goomble-Gubbon" from LIFE IN THE DESERTS by Lucy Baker. Copyright © 1990 by Two-Can Publishing Ltd. Used by permission.

Poems and Songs 24: "When I First Came to This Land," words and music by Oscar Brand. TRO © copyright 1957 (Renewed), 1965 (Renewed) Ludlow Music, Inc., New York, New York. Used by permission. 38: "Comida/Food" by Victor M. Valle from FIESTA IN AZTLAN. Reprinted by permission of Capra Press. 52: "What a Wonderful World" by Bob Thiele and George David Weiss. 114: "On the Road Again," words and music by Willie Nelson. Copyright © 1979 by Full Nelson Music, Inc. All rights administered by Windswept Pacific Entertainment Co. d/b/a/ Longitude Music Co. All rights reserved. Used by permission of Warner Bros. Publications U.S. Inc., Miami, FL 33014. 152: "Blame," from A LIGHT IN THE ATTIC by Shel Silverstein. Copyright © 1981 by Evil Eye Music, Inc. Reprinted by permission of HarperCollins Publishers. 176: "The Happy Wanderer" by Antonia Ridge. 190: "Watching Gray Whales" by J. S. Baird. Reprinted by permission. 214: "The Desert," words and music by Malvina Reynolds. Copyright © 1960 by Schroder Music Co. (ASCAP), renewed 1988. Used by permission. All rights reserved. 228: "Cool Water" by Bob Nolan. Warner Bros. Music.

Photography Unless otherwise acknowledged, all photographs are the property of Scott, Foresman and Company. Page abbreviations are as follows: (t) top, (c) center, (b) bottom, (r) right.

v (t) Beryl Goldberg, (bl) Civic Library of Padua/Superstock, Inc., (br)David Young-Wolff/PhotoEdit; 2-3(b) Lawrence Migdale/Stock Boston; 3(c) Superstock, Inc.; (t) Jose Carrillo/PhotoEdit; 4 Pilgrim Society; 5(b) Jeff Greenberg/PhotoEdit; (t) Library of Congress; (c) Cameramann International, Ltd.; 26 Joe Viesti; 27(bl) David Austen/Tony Stone Images; (tl, tr) Beryl Goldberg; (br) Superstock, Inc.; 28(cr) Bob Child/Wide World; (t) Archive Photos; (cl) Darlene Hammond/Archive Photos; (b) Zade Rosenthal/Archive Photos; 29(tl, bl) Wide World; (br) Paul Burnett/Wide World; 30(r) William A. Allard/National Geographic; (l) Bowers Museum of Cultural Art; 31(t, b) Superstock, Inc.; 32(l) Martha Cooper/Viesti Associates, Inc. ; 32–33(b) Cameramann/Image Works; 33(t) David Ryan/DDB Stock Photos; 40(b) Anna E. Zuckerman/PhotoEdit; 41(t) Superstock, Inc.; (b) Private Collection/Superstock, Inc.; 45 Lennart Nilsson; 51 ©1977 David Scharf/Peter Arnold, Inc.; 55(b) David Young-Wolff/PhotoEdit; (t) Superstock, Inc.; 56(l, r), Comstock Inc.; (c) Tony Stone Images; 57(r) Comstock Inc.; (l) Norbert Wu/Peter Arnold, Inc.; 58 Runk/Schoenberger/Grant Heilman Photography; 59 Peter Arnold, Inc.; 62(b) Courtesy Greenberg, Van Doren Gallery/Photograph by Steven Sloman; (t) Art Institute of Chicago/Superstock, Inc.; 63(b) Superstock, Inc.; (t) Christie's, London/Superstock, Inc.; 78(t, b) Granger Collection, New York; 79(t) Victoria & Albert Museum, London/Superstock, Inc.; (b) British Library, London/A.K.G. Berlin/Superstock, Inc.; 80(b) Bibliotheque Nationale, Paris/E.T. Archives, London/Superstock, Inc.; (t) British Library, London/Bridgeman Art Library, London/Superstock, Inc.; 81(t) Civic Library of Padua/Superstock, Inc.; (tl) Granger Collection, New York; (bl) Alinari/Art Resource; 82(t) Superstock, Inc.; (b) Erich Lessing/Art Resource; 83(t) British Library, London/Superstock, Inc.; (b) Erich Lessing/Art Resource; 84(l, r) Granger Collection, New York; 85(tl) Erich Lessing/Art Resource; (tr) The Pierpont Morgan Library/Art Resource; 86(t) Metropolitan Museum of Art, The Cloisters Collection, 1947. (47.101.51) Photograph by Lynton Gardiner.; (b) The Pierpont Morgan Library/Art Resource; 102 Superstock, Inc.; 103(t) Collegio del Cambio, Perugia/Superstock, Inc.; (b) Giraudon/Art Resource; (c) Scala/Art Resource; 104(r) Biblioteca Estense, Modena/Superstock, Inc.; (l) Granger Collection, New York; 105(t) Superstock, Inc.; 105(c, b), 107, 108(t, b), 109(r) Granger Collection, New York; 111(t) Superstock, Inc.; (b) Granger Collection, New York; 112 Photo by Skira/National Palace Museum, China; 115 Granger Collection, New York; 117(t) Sidney Harris; 138 Metropolitan Museum of Art, Arthur Hoppock Hearn Fund, 1958, (58.26); 140(t, br) Beryl Goldberg; (bl) © 1993 Jason Lauré/Black Star; 141, 142 Beryl Goldberg; 148 Bill Gallery/Stock Boston; 149(b) Courtesy of Laura Dail; 154(t, b), 154–155 (background), 155(t, b) Superstock, Inc.; 156 Tony Morrison/South American Pictures; 157(b) Robert Frerck/Odyssey Productions; (tl, tr) Boltin Picture Library; 158(bl, br) Tony Morrison/South American Pictures; 158(t), 159(t) Mike Pepper/Odyssey Productions; (b) Robert Frerck/Odyssey Productions; 160 Superstock, Inc.; (t) Boltin Picture Library; 161 Mary Jane Maples; 162(t, b) Superstock, Inc.; (inset) Robert Francis/South American Pictures; 163(t, b), 164 Superstock, Inc.; 165 Tony Morrison/South American Pictures; 166–167 Robert Frerck/Odyssey Productions; 167(t), 168(t) Tony Morrison/South American Pictures; (b), 169 Robert Frerck/Odyssey Productions; 170(t) Superstock, Inc.; 171 Robert Frerck/Odyssey Productions; 172, 173, 174(tl) Tony Morrison/South American Pictures; (b) Robert Frerck/Odyssey Productions; (tr) Boltin Picture Library; 175(b) Tony Morrison/South American Pictures; (t) Robert Frerck/Odyssey Productions; 177 Superstock, Inc.; 178(t) USGS/TSADO/Tom Stack & Associates; (b) Eugene G. Schulz; 179(b) Superstock, Inc.; (t) Photri; 180(t) Michael Nolan/Tom Stack & Associates; (b) Gerald & Buff Corsi/Tom Stack & Associates; 181(t) W. Perry Conway/Tom Stack & Associates; (b) Superstock, Inc.; (c) K. Glaser & Associates/Custom Medical Stock Photo; 184 Photri, Inc.; 188 Hulton Deutsch Collection Ltd.; 189(b) Mary Evans Picture Library; (t) Hulton Deutsch Collection Ltd.; 191 Photri; 193(r) Superstock, Inc.; (l) Wolfgang Kaehler; 196(b) Superstock, Inc.; (t) Zig Leszczynski/Animals Animals; 197(r) Joe McDonald/Tom Stack & Associates; (l), 198, 200 Superstock, Inc.; 201 Robert Frerck/Odyssey Productions; 216 Partridge Films Limited/Oxford Scientific Films/Earth Scenes; 217(b) Jane Lewis/Tony Stone Images; (t) Doug Sokell/Tom Stack & Associates; 218 Joe McDonald/Animals Animals; 219 Superstock, Inc.; 220(t) Nicholas DeVore/Tony Stone Images; (c, b) Superstock, Inc.; 221(t) Jane Lewis/Tony Stone Images; 222 Bob Pool/Tom Stack & Associates; 223 Don & Pat Valenti/Tony Stone Images; 229 Joe McDonald/Animals Animals.

CRITIC READERS

Sandra H. Bible
Elementary ESL Teacher
Shawnee Mission School District
Shawnee Mission, Kansas

Betty A. Billups
Dallas Independent School District
Dallas, Texas

María G. Cano
BIL/ESL Specialist
Pasadena Independent School District
Pasadena, Texas

Anaida Colón-Muñiz, Ed.D.
Director of English Language
 Development and Bilingual
 Education
Santa Ana Unified School District
Santa Ana, California

Debbie Corkey-Corber
Educational Consultant
Williamsburg, Virginia

Lily Pham Dam
Instructional Specialist
Dallas Independent School District
Dallas, Texas

María Delgado
Edison Middle School
Milwaukee Public Schools
Milwaukee, Wisconsin

Dr. M. Viramontes de Marín
Chair, Education/Liberal Arts
 Departments
The National Hispanic University
San Jose,California

Timothy Hart
Supervisor of English as a
 Second Language
Wake County
Raleigh, North Carolina

Lilian I. Jezik
Bilingual Resource Teacher
Colorna-Norco Unified School District
Norco, California

Helen L. Lin
Chairman, Education Program
Multicultural Arts Council of
 Orange County, California
Formerly ESL Lab Director,
 Kansas City, Kansas, Schools

Teresa Montaño
United Teachers Los Angeles
Los Angeles, California

Loriana M. Novoa, Ed.D.
Research and Evaluation Consultants
Miami, Florida

Rosa María Peña
Austin Independent School District
Austin, Texas

Thuy Pham-Remmele
ESL/Bilingual K–12 Specialist
Madison Metropolitan School District
Madison, Wisconsin

Roberto San Miguel
Kennedy-Zapata Elementary School
El Cenizo, Texas

Jacqueline J. Servi Margis
ESL and Foreign Language
 Curriculum Specialist
Milwaukee Public Schools
Milwaukee, Wisconsin

Elizabeth Streightoff
ESL Magnet Teacher,
 Lamar Elementary School
Conroe Independent School District
The Woodlands, Texas

Lydia M. Trujillo
Hot Topics Consultants
Pueblo, Colorado

Susan C. VanLeuven
Poudre R-1 School District
Fort Collins, Colorado

Rosaura Villaseñor, M.A.
Educator
Norwalk, California

Sharon Weiss
ESL Consultant
Glenview, Illinois

Cheryl Wilkinson
J. O. Davis Elementary School
Irving Independent School District
Irving, Texas

Phyllis I. Ziegler
ESL/Bilingual Consultant
New York, New York

TABLE OF CONTENTS

Journeys to New Lands

Word Bank

education
fun
home
job
money
safety

Tell what you know.

Why do people make journeys?

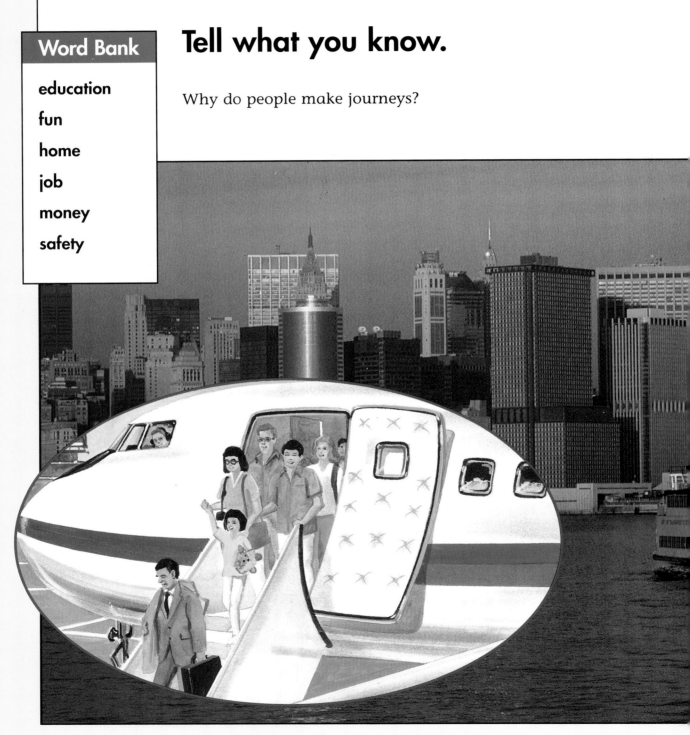

Talk About It

Tell about a journey you have taken. Where did your journey begin? Where did you go? Why did you go?

3

Immigration Then and Now

Why do people immigrate?

Throughout history, people have moved to new places. People who move to a new country to live are called **immigrants**.

Why do people leave their native countries? Sometimes they can't find jobs in their country. They move to get jobs and have a better life. These people move for **economic reasons.**

Sometimes people can't practice their religion in their native country. They move for **religious reasons.**

Sometimes countries are at war. People move to a new country to be safe. They move for **political reasons.**

Talk About It

Why did your family immigrate?

What new things do immigrants find in a new land?

The First Immigrants to North America

People have lived in the Americas for thousands of years. American Indians lived throughout North and South America.

The Indians came from Asia thousands of years ago. They settled throughout North and South America.

In the 1500s and 1600s, people started immigrating to North America from Europe. Many came from England and Spain.

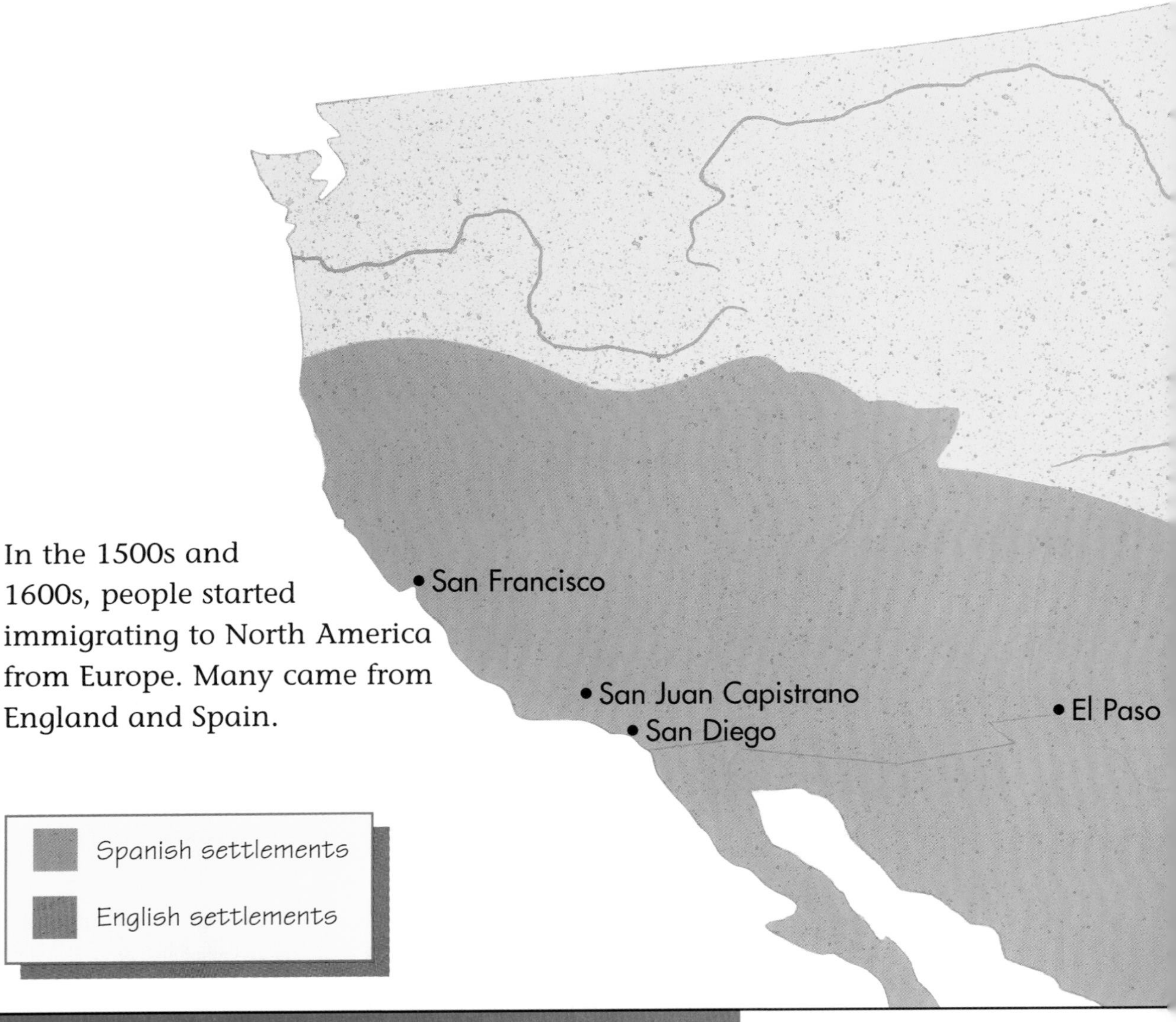

• San Francisco

• San Juan Capistrano
• San Diego

• El Paso

Spanish settlements

English settlements

Many of the English immigrants came for religious reasons. They wanted to practice their religion. Many of the Spanish immigrants came for economic reasons. They wanted to find treasure and adventure.

Some people did not want to leave their homes. Beginning in the 1600s, Africans were brought to the Americas as slaves.

Boston
Plymouth
New York
Philadelphia
Williamsburg
Jamestown
Norfolk
Charleston
St. Augustine
Pensacola
San Antonio

Think About It

Why do you think the English settled where they did? Why do you think the Spanish settled where they did?

Later Immigrants to the United States

Starting in the 1800s, huge numbers of immigrants came to the United States.

Most of these immigrants came from Europe. They came from countries such as Italy, Russia, Ireland, and Germany. Other immigrants came from countries in Asia such as Japan and China.

Many of these immigrants came for economic reasons. They were looking for better jobs and a better life.

Immigrants are still coming to the United States. Many immigrants today come from Asian countries such as Vietnam. Many more come from Latin American countries such as Mexico.

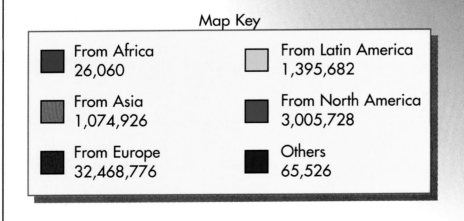

Map Key

■	From Africa 26,060	▢	From Latin America 1,395,682
▨	From Asia 1,074,926	■	From North America 3,005,728
■	From Europe 32,468,776	■	Others 65,526

Immigration to the United States 1820-1940

Talk About It

What do the arrows on this map mean? Which is the widest arrow? Which arrows are narrower? What do the differences tell you about immigrants who came to the United States?

Chart the immigration numbers.

These pie charts show information about where immigrants lived before they came to the United States.

These charts show the changes in the **percentage** of immigrants arriving in the United States from different continents. Each pie chart totals 100% of the immigrants who came during the years shown in the title of the chart.

Immigration to U.S.

2% Other

1% Africa

4% Asia

16% North America

21% Latin America

56% Europe

1931 – 1960

Try It Out

Below are the percentages of immigrants from different continents who came to the United States from 1981 to 1990. Make a pie chart with these percentages. Color the percentages for each continent. Use the same colors for the continents as those in the pie charts.

1981–1990

Africa	3%	Latin America	47%
Asia	38%	North America	2%
Europe	9%	Other	1%

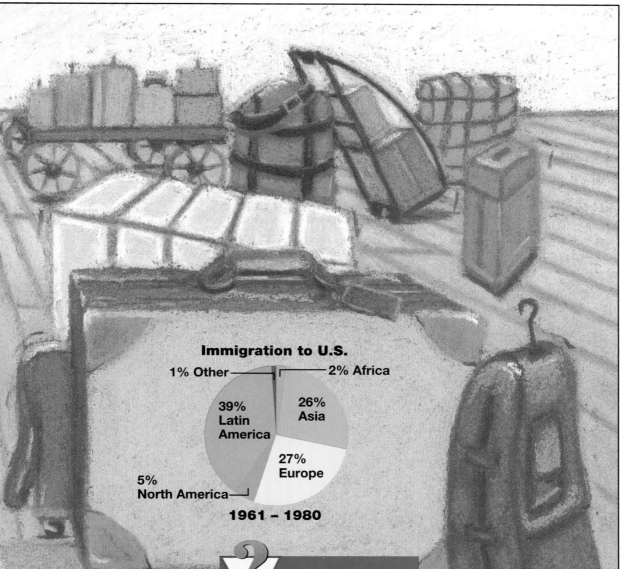

Immigration to U.S.

1% Other

2% Africa

39% Latin America

26% Asia

27% Europe

5% North America

1961 – 1980

Think About It

Compare the pie pieces of the same color with one another. How do they change over the three charts?

Which percentages increased (got larger)? Why do you think this happened?

Which percentages decreased (got smaller)? Why do you think this happened?

How Many Days to America?

by Eve Bunting
illustrated by
Beth Peck

Reader's Tip
The family in this story is leaving their country for political reasons. When the story begins, they have left their home and are waiting on a boat. The young son of the family is telling the story.

"How many days to America?" my little sister asked.

"Not many," my father said. "Don't be afraid."

The fishing boat was small and there were many people. More kept coming, and more. We chugged heavily from harbor to open ocean.

"Can we see America yet, Papa?" All the *time* my little sister asks questions.

"Not yet," my father said.

We were an hour from shore when the motors stopped.

The men crowded the engines.

"A part is broken that cannot be fixed," my father told my mother, and her face twisted the way it did when she closed the door of our home for the last time.

The women made a sail by knotting clothes together and when they pulled it high I saw my Father's Sunday shirt blowing in the wind. But the sail carried us back toward our own shore and men shot at us from the cliffs.

At last we got the boat turned in the right direction.

"How many days to America now?" my little sister asked.

"More, my small one," my father said and he held us close. I saw him look at my mother across our heads.

Study Tips
Characters' Problems
In stories, characters often have problems. As you read, look for the problems to understand what is happening in the story. What problems does the family in the story have on their journey?

Language Tip
Idiom
Run out means that there isn't any more of something. The people on the boat have no more food and water.

Study Tips
Stop and Think
Imagine what the characters must be feeling as things happen to them. What do you think the people in the boat are feeling as they sail toward America? Look for clues in the story.

Day followed night and night, day. Our food and water ran out and many people were sick.

At sunset, my father and mother and sister and I huddled in the bow. Then my father sang as he sang at home.

"Sleep and dream, tomorrow comes
And we shall all be free."

That was the only time I was not afraid.

By day we fished and shared the catch. When it rained we caught the water in our buckets. I slept and dreamed. Of home. Of food. Of my favorite uncle who worked with my father in his shop and who had stayed behind. Sometimes I cried and then my mother would rock me against her.

Once we saw a whale, gray as an elephant and covered with barnacles.

"Come push us, whale," my mother called. "Push us to America."

But the whale did not hear.

Language Tip
Vocabulary
Barnacles are small shellfish. They often grow on larger fish or boats.

Once there was a shout of "Land!" and we crowded the railing. But though we pulled on the sail our boat would go no closer.

"We will swim for help," my father said and he and two others jumped into the water.

"No!" my mother cried.

But they were gone already.

When at last we saw them rise on the green roll of the surf, saw them carried to shore, we danced and cheered.

But there were soldiers on the rocks.

Everyone was quiet and my mother gripped my hand.

"They are bringing them back," she whispered. Three soldiers with rifles came too, in the small boat. They brought us water and fruit, but they did not speak or smile as they tossed it up to our waiting hands.

"Was it not the right land, Papa?" I asked as the soldiers pulled away. "Will it not do?"

"It would do. But they will not take us," my father said.

My sister tugged at his arm. "They don't like us?"

"It is not that." He did not explain what it was.

Reader's Tip
Stop and Think
Some countries do not accept immigrants. Why do you think this is so?

Language Tip
Vocabulary
A papaya is a sweet
fruit of a tropical tree.

Reader's Tip
Stop and Think
Why do you think the
young boy was "afraid
to hope"?

Our family got two papayas and three lemons and a coconut with milk that tasted like flowers.

The sea was rough that night and my father's song lost itself in the wind. I said the words as the stars dipped and turned above our heads.

"Tomorrow comes, tomorrow comes,
And we shall all be free."

It was the next day, the tomorrow, that we sighted land again. I was afraid to hope.

A boat came. My mother clasped her hands and bent her head. Was she afraid to hope too?

The boat circled us twice and then a line was thrown and we were pulled toward shore.

There was such a silence among us then, such an anxious, watchful silence.

People waited on the dock.

"Welcome," they called. "Welcome to America."

Reader's Tip
Thanksgiving is a holiday in the United States in November. It honors a time in 1621 when the first English settlers and Native Americans shared food and came together to celebrate the harvest.

That was when our silence turned to cheers.

"But how did they know we would come today?" my father asked.

"Perhaps people come every day," my mother said. "Perhaps they understand how it is for us."

There was a shed, warm from the sun on its tin roof. There were tables covered with food. Though the benches were crowded there was room for all of us.

"Do you know what day this is?" a woman asked me. She passed me a dinner plate.

"It is the coming-to-America day," I said.

She smiled. "Yes. And it is special for another reason, too. Today is Thanksgiving."

"What is that?" My little sister was shy, but not too shy to ask her questions.

"Long ago, unhappy people came here to start new lives," the woman said. "They celebrated by giving thanks."

My father nodded. "That is the only true way to celebrate."

When I First Came to This Land

by Oscar Brand

When I first came to this land
I was not a wealthy man
So I got myself a shack and I did what I could
And I called my shack: "Break my back"
But the land was sweet and good
and I did what I could

When I first came to this land
I was not a wealthy man
So I got myself a wife and I did what I could
And I called my wife: "Joy of My Life"
But the land was sweet and good
and I did what I could

Write About It

Write a song or poem that begins, "When I first came to this land. . ."

Tell what you learned.

1. Why did the early immigrants come to the Americas?

2. List reasons people immigrate. Can you think of any other reasons?

3. How was your journey to America different from or similar to the one in the story?

4. Interview someone who has immigrated to the United States. Why did the person move? How did the person feel?

Gifts from Many Lands

Tell what you know.

Every immigrant group brings things from its native country to its new country.

How many can you name?

Word Bank

art

food

games

music

religion

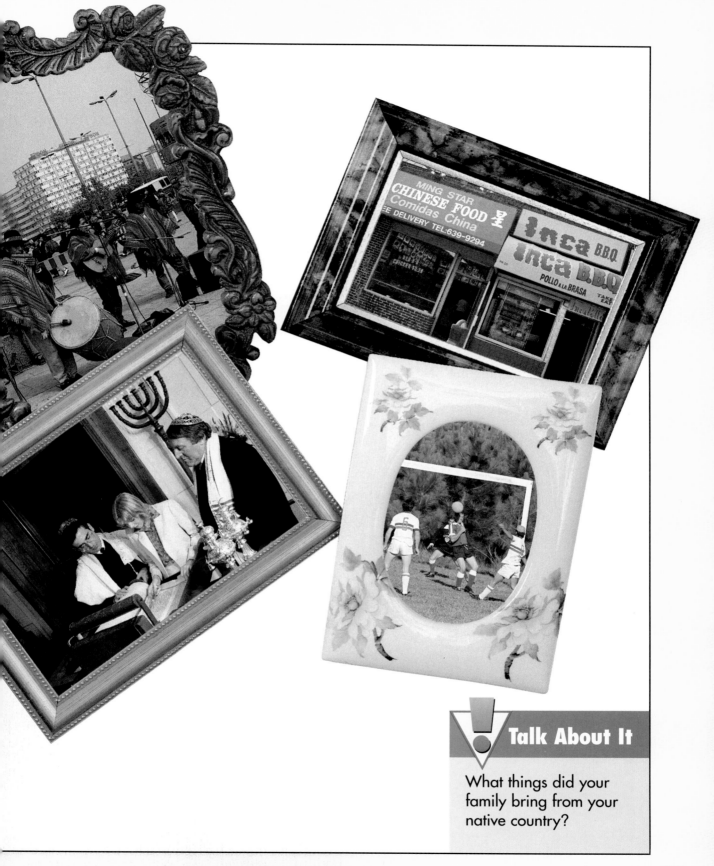

Talk About It

What things did your family bring from your native country?

27

Famous Immigrants

Immigrants bring their own personal talents to their new countries. They enrich the lives of others who live there.

Monica Seles is a famous tennis ▶ player. She was born in the former Yugoslavia in 1973. At seventeen, she became the best woman tennis player in the world. She became a United States citizen in 1994.

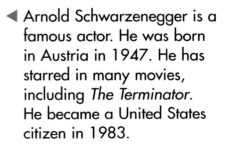

◀ Arnold Schwarzenegger is a famous actor. He was born in Austria in 1947. He has starred in many movies, including *The Terminator*. He became a United States citizen in 1983.

◄ Isabel Allende is a famous novelist. She was born in Peru in 1942. She has written many novels, including *The House of the Spirits* and *The Stories of Eva Luna*. She moved to the United States in 1988.

I.M. Pei is a famous architect. ► He was born in China in 1917. He has designed many buildings, including the Rock and Roll Hall of Fame in Cleveland, Ohio. He became a United States citizen in 1954.

Talk About It

Have any of these famous immigrants enriched your life? How?

Name other immigrants who have enriched your life. How have they done so?

Learning from One Another

People learn from one another. They borrow **customs** and language from other groups.

The early Spanish settlers brought horses to North America. They used the horses on their cattle ranches. Workers on the ranches were called *vaqueros.*

Vaqueros wore pieces of leather over their pants to protect their legs. They wore hats with wide brims to protect themselves from rain and sun.

When settlers from the eastern part of the United States went west in the 1800s, they saw how the *vaqueros* lived and worked. When these settlers began to raise cattle, they borrowed customs and language from the *vaqueros*. The customs and language became part of the cowboy way of life.

Many cowboy words come from Spanish. Look at the chart.

Spanish	English	Meaning
chaperejos	chaps	leather covering worn over pants
corral	corral	fenced area for horses or cattle
la reata	lariat	rope for catching horses or cattle
rancho	ranch	large cattle, sheep, or horse farm
rodear	rodeo	cowboy show

? Think About It

Are English words used in your language? What are they? Why do you think they are used?

Are any words from your language used in English? Why do you think they are used?

We celebrate together.

When people immigrate to a new place, they bring their **celebrations** with them. A celebration often has special food and music.

Chinese Americans celebrate the beginning of their new year in late winter or early spring. People hold parades with fireworks and a huge dragon. Many Americans who are not of Chinese origin enjoy the parades.

Irish Americans celebrate St. Patrick's Day on March 17 to honor Ireland's special saint. People hold parties and parades. They wear green and remember Ireland. Many people who are not of Irish origin celebrate St. Patrick's Day. There is a saying, "Everyone is Irish on St. Patrick's Day."

Mexican Americans celebrate *Cinco de Mayo* (May 5). This holiday honors a Mexican military victory. People hold parades and festivals. Many people who are not of Mexican origin enjoy the music and dancing.

Think About It

Which celebrations did you and your family bring with you from your native country? What do you do during those celebrations?

Name some other holidays that you have learned about since you have come to the United States.

Who named it?

Place names in the United States can sometimes tell about the people who first settled an area.

Some places in the United States were named by American Indians. For example, the state of Utah gets its name from the Ute people who lived there.

English settlers named many places in the East. They often added the word *new* to the name of a place in England. That's how New York and New Jersey got their names.

Des Moines, IOWA
5 MILES

Thank You For Visiting CAIRO, ILLINOIS

STUYVESANT PARK
HISTORICAL SITE

YOU ARE NOW ENTERING THE STATE OF CALIFORNIA

GREAT PLACES
HIGHWAY USA

The Spanish settlers named many places in the West and South. Los Angeles means *the angels* in Spanish, and San Antonio, in Texas, is named for a Christian saint.

Some places get their names from famous immigrants. Streets named Pulaski or Kosciusko, for example, honor military heroes who came from Poland.

WELCOME TO THE STATE OF UTAH

BUENA VISTA AVE

City Of MOSCOW, INDIANA

SCOTCH PLAINS NEW JERSEY

SUSQUEHANNA RIVER

NEW YORK CITY

? Think About It

If you could name the street you live on for someone from your native country, what name would you choose?

Delicious Differences

Americans enjoy food from many parts of the world. Here are recipes for sauces from the Middle East and Mexico. Dip tortilla chips, pita bread, or crackers into the sauces, and you will have a tasty snack.

MIDDLE EASTERN HUMMUS DIP

1 clove garlic
1/2 cup parsley
1 16-ounce can
   chickpeas
1 tablespoon tahini
   (sesame seed paste)
juice from 1 lemon
1 tablespoon olive oil

1. Peel and chop garlic. Chop parsley.
2. Blend ingredients in blender.
3. Serve with pita bread.

Mexican Salsa

2 ripe tomatoes
1 pickled jalapeño chili pepper
1 onion
1 clove garlic
2 tablespoons vegetable oil
1/2 teaspoon sugar
1/2 teaspoon ground cilantro
   (coriander)
salt and pepper

1. Peel the tomatoes and remove the seeds. Then chop them. Remove the seeds from the jalapeño pepper. Chop it. Peel and chop the garlic and onion.

2. Combine the tomatoes, onion, garlic, and jalapeño pepper. Add vegetable oil, sugar, cilantro, salt, and pepper. Stir.

3. Serve with tortillas or tortilla chips.

Write About It

Do you ever eat foods that come from other countries? Which ones have you eaten? What is your favorite food from another country?

Comida/Food

by Victor M. Valle

Uno se come
la luna en la tortilla
Comes frijol
y comes tierra
Comes chile
y comes sol y fuego
Bebes agua
y bebes cielo

One eats
the moon in a tortilla
Eat frijoles
and you eat the earth
Eat chile
and you eat sun and fire
Drink water
and you drink sky

? Think About It

Find out about the foods listed in the poem. How is a tortilla like the moon? How are frijoles (beans) like the earth? How is chile like the sun and fire? How is water like the sky?

Tell what you learned.

1. What kinds of things do immigrant groups bring to the United States?

2. What have you learned about another immigrant group since you have been in the United States? Tell about it.

3. Have you ever attended another immigrant group's celebration or festival? What did you do? Write a letter to a friend about it.

Sight and Color

Word Bank

art

movies

photographs

scenery

videos

Tell what you know.

How many ways do people use their eyes?

Talk About It

What is your favorite thing to look at? What if you couldn't see it? Would you miss seeing it?

41

How the Eyes Work

How do the parts of the eye work?

The parts of the eye work together so we can see.

Study the pictures that show the parts of the eye.

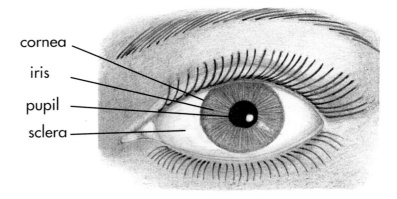

cornea
iris
pupil
sclera

The white part of the eye is called the **sclera.** It is a tough cover that protects the eye.

The front of the eye is covered by the **cornea.** The cornea is clear so that light can go through it. The cornea covers the **iris,** the colored part of the eye. The iris controls how much light enters the eye.

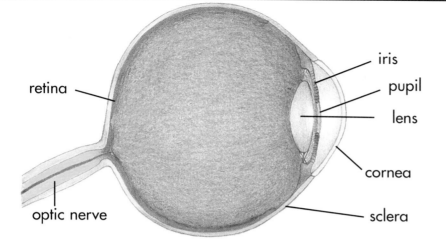

retina

iris

pupil

lens

cornea

sclera

optic nerve

The black dot in the middle of the iris is the **pupil.** It is an opening to the inside of the eye. Light enters the eye through the pupil.

Behind the **pupil,** inside the eye, is the **lens.** Light shines through the lens onto the **retina.** The retina is a thin lining on the back of the eyeball. It is connected to the optic nerve. The **optic nerve** carries pictures from the eye to the brain.

Word Bank

film

iris

lens

photograph

shutter

Think About It

The camera has some parts that do the same things an eye does. Which parts do you think they are?

What happens when we look at something?

Imagine that you are outside on a sunny day. A friend across the street waves to you. Light from the sun shines on your friend. Light **reflects,** or bounces, from your friend to you. The light enters your eyes through the pupil.

Light then goes through the lens of the eye. The lens changes its shape to help you **focus,** or see a clear, sharp picture of your friend. The lens bends the reflected light and focuses the light on the retina. A picture of your friend forms on the retina like a picture on a movie screen. But the picture on the retina is upside down.

The retina is made of **rods** and **cones.** These tiny organs help you see shapes and colors. The cones help you see the color of the clothing your friend is wearing.

The retina then sends the picture of your friend to your brain. Your brain turns the picture right side up, and you see your friend.

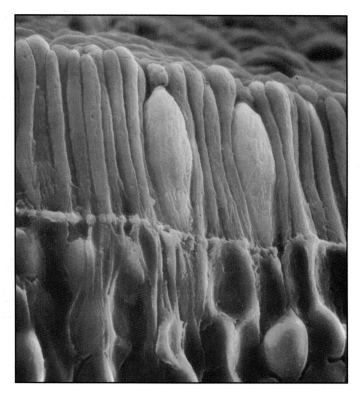

◀ Rods and cones are tiny organs in the retina. Cones help you see colors. Rods help you see black and white.

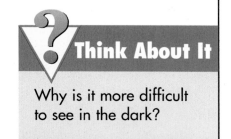

Think About It

Why is it more difficult to see in the dark?

How do two eyes work together?

Why do you have two eyes? Why wouldn't one big eye be just as good? Two eyes allow you to see more things and to see them more clearly.

Both eyes have to work together to give you **depth perception.** Depth perception is the ability to see the space between and around objects at a distance.

How do two eyes create depth perception? Use these steps to help you find out how your eyes work together.

1. Hold a pencil at arm's length.

2. Focus your eyes on the pencil.

3. First close one eye. Then quickly open it and close your other eye.

4. Repeat step 3 several times.

What do you notice? What happens to the pencil?

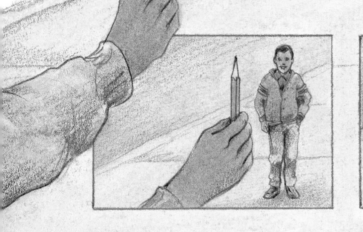

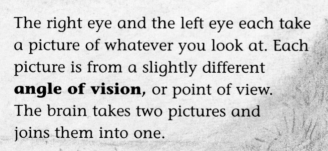

The right eye and the left eye each take a picture of whatever you look at. Each picture is from a slightly different **angle of vision,** or point of view. The brain takes two pictures and joins them into one.

Talk About It

What did the experiment show you about how people see?

Talking About Eyes

Idioms are expressions with special meanings.

Saying that a person *has a green thumb* is an idiom. People use this idiom to say that a person is good at growing plants. That person's thumb isn't *really* green!

There are many idioms in English about eyes and seeing. Here are just a few.

Crying your eyes out means to cry hard. ▶
Mira cried her eyes out when she found out her family was moving to another city.

◀ **Seeing eye to eye** means to agree.
My sister and I don't always see eye to eye.

Keep an eye on means to watch ▶ someone carefully.
Shanti really had to keep an eye on little Raymond.

To pull the wool over someone's eyes is to fool someone.
Peter did not find out about the surprise birthday party for him. Habib really pulled the wool over his eyes!

◀ **In the wink of an eye** means very quickly.
In the wink of an eye, Hiro was gone.

▼ **Keep your eyes on the prize** means keep your goals in mind as you work.
While Lillian studied for her tests, she said, "I need to keep my eyes on the prize."

Write About It

Record any other English idioms that you know on index cards. Add new idioms as you learn them.

Different Kinds of Eyes

Bees have some of the most interesting eyes in nature. Why? Because bees, like some other insects, have compound eyes. The word *compound* means "with more than one part." A bee's compound eye has more than 6,000 tiny lenses. A human eye has only one lens.

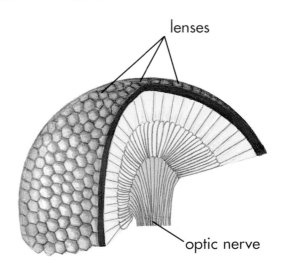

lenses

optic nerve

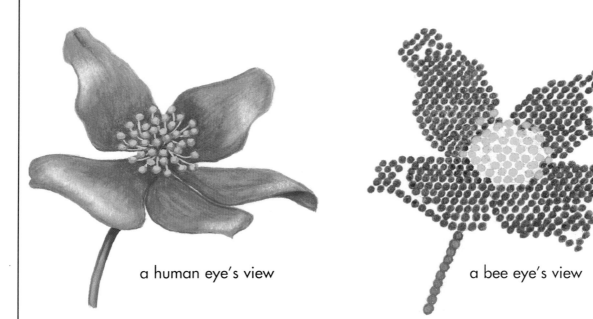

a human eye's view

a bee eye's view

The view from a bee's eye is very different from the view from a human eye. When a bee looks at a flower, each lens in the bee's eye sees only a tiny part of the flower. Every lens sends a picture to the brain. So a bee sees a flower as a pattern made up of many pieces. A bee does not see a clear, sharp picture of a flower as a human does.

Scientists think that compound eyes help insects such as bees see movement better. When an object moves, it appears in one lens after the other. The series of pictures makes moving objects easier to see. This helps bees escape enemies.

With their special eyes, bees can also see a kind of light humans can't see. Many flowers reflect this kind of light. This helps bees locate these flowers and get food from them.

Bees have compound eyes with many lenses.

a human eye's view

a bee eye's view

Think About It

How do a bee's eyes help it survive?

What a Wonderful World

by George David Weiss and Bob Thiele

I see trees of green, red roses too,
I see them bloom for me and you,
and I think to myself
What a wonderful world.
The colors of the rainbow, so pretty in the sky
are also on the faces of people goin' by,
I see friends shakin' hands, sayin', "How do you do!"
They're really sayin' "I love you,"
I hear babies cry, I watch them grow
They'll learn much more than I'll ever know
and I think to myself
What a wonderful world.
Yes, I think to myself
What a wonderful world.

Talk About It

Name some things that the song says are wonderful. Do you agree with the song? What is something you think is wonderful about the world?

Tell what you learned.

1. Draw a diagram of the human eye. Label the parts.

2. You see an airplane in the sky. Explain how your eyes are able to see it.

3. What is the most interesting fact you learned about eyes in this chapter?

Looking at Colors

Tell what you know.

Color is all around us. How many colors can you name?

What colors do you see in nature?
What colors do you see people wearing? What colors do you see at celebrations?

Colors affect how we feel. How do the colors in these pictures make you feel?

MATH TIME

Celebrate Reading!

A VOLCANO OF CHEERS

Talk About It

What colors do you like best? What colors don't you like?

What colors do you like to wear?

55

What is light?

Light is one kind of **radiant energy.** Think about sunlight, for example. It is actually a kind of energy. It provides the earth with heat as well as light.

Have you seen waves move in water? Radiant energy moves in the same way that waves do. But most kinds of radiant energy cannot be seen by the human eye.

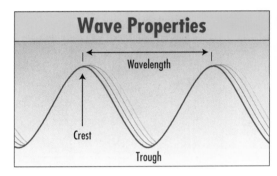

Look at the graph on this page. The distance from the top of one wave to the top of the next wave is called a **wavelength.** Different kinds of radiant energy have different wavelengths.

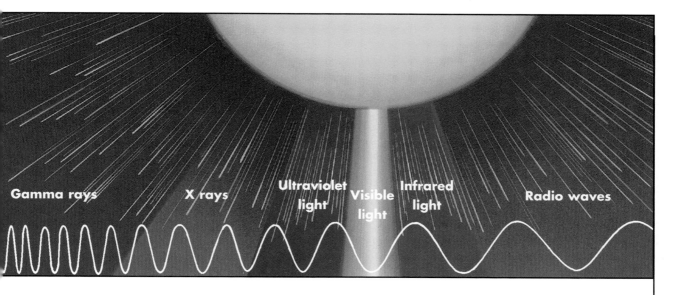

Gamma rays   X rays   Ultraviolet light   Visible light   Infrared light   Radio waves

The chart on this page shows the different kinds of radiant energy. Another name for them is the **electromagnetic spectrum.** Light is the only part of the spectrum people can see. Light is the visible part of the spectrum. Other parts of this spectrum are radio and TV signals, microwaves, and X rays.

Light seems to be white, but it is made of seven different colors. Each color has its own wavelength. Red light has the longest wavelength, and violet light has the shortest wavelength.

Talk About It

What kinds of light do you see every day? How do you use light? Why do you need light?

Where do rainbows come from?

Light is made of many colors. The colors of the rainbow are red, orange, yellow, green, blue, indigo, and violet.

One way to make light show all its colors is to shine it through a **prism.** When light passes into the prism, the light waves bend. This bending of light waves is called **refraction.** As the light passes out of the prism, it is bent again.

This second bending of the light causes the light to separate into different colors. This happens because some wavelengths of light bend more than others.

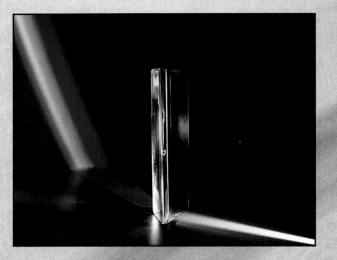

▲ Light shines through a prism, and it spreads out into the colors of the rainbow.

red   orange   yellow   green   blue   indigo   violet

When you see a rainbow in the sky, it is caused by the sun shining through water droplets in the air. The water droplets are acting like tiny prisms. They cause the light to refract. The light spreads apart into the **spectrum,** the colors of a rainbow.

▲ Light *refracts* through water droplets to make a rainbow.

Talk About It

Have you ever seen a rainbow?

People in some places see a rainbow as something good. It can bring good luck. Why do you think people have this opinion about rainbows?

Make a rainbow.

You have learned how prisms and water droplets make rainbows. Here's how to make your own rainbow. Look at the pictures as you follow the steps.

Things You Need

a shallow bowl

water

a small mirror

a lump of clay or a stone

sunlight

a white wall or large sheet of white paper

Follow these steps.

1. Fill the bowl with water.

2. Put the bowl in the sunlight.

3. Put a small mirror into the bowl. Use the clay or stone to make the mirror stand up against the side of the bowl.

4. Move the bowl or mirror so the sunlight reflects onto a white wall or paper. What do you see?

Together the mirror and the water act like a prism. They cause the light to refract into the seven colors of the spectrum.

My Record

What I did in this experiment:

What colors I saw:

What order they were in:

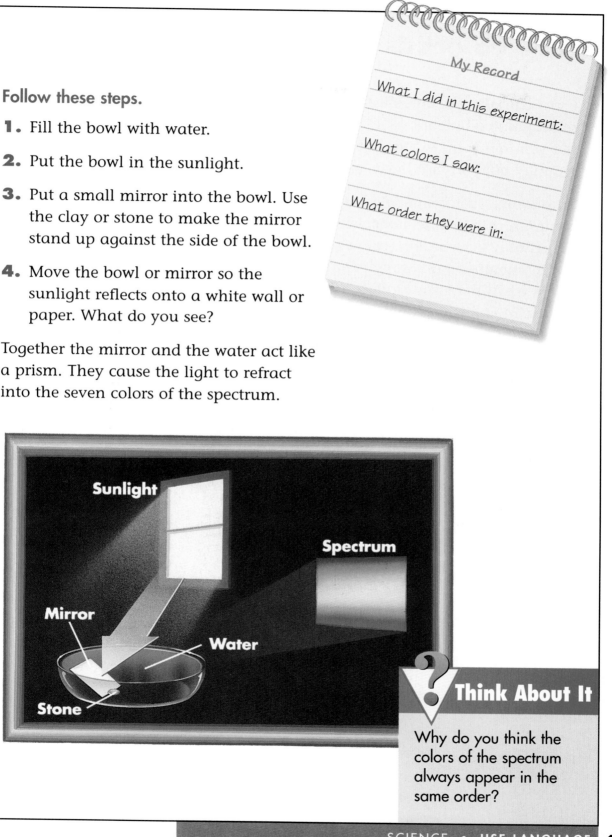

Sunlight

Spectrum

Mirror

Water

Stone

Think About It

Why do you think the colors of the spectrum always appear in the same order?

How do artists use color?

Color can affect people's feelings, or **moods.** A room painted blue may feel cool and quiet, and put you in a calm mood. The same room painted red may put you in a lively, energetic mood.

Throughout history, people have used color to communicate their feelings. In some places, it is the custom to wear dark colors when a friend or family member dies. Many people wear bright colors when they want to feel more cheerful and happy. In English, people say "I'm feeling blue" to tell that they are sad.

▲ How do the colors in this painting make you feel? Why?

◀ This artwork is made of pieces of painted metal. How would the artwork be different if the artist had used different colors?

Many artists use color to create a mood in a work of art. Sometimes they want you to feel a special mood when you look at their artwork. What moods do you think these artists are creating with the colors in the pictures on these two pages?

◀ Why do you think the artist used only a few colors in this painting?

Word Bank

calm

excited

happy

relaxed

sad

tired

Try It Out

Make a list of colors. Write how they make you feel.

Trade papers with a partner. Do you have some of the same feelings about colors?

Then choose a mood. Draw a picture to illustrate that mood.

The River That Gave Gifts

Written and Illustrated by Margo Humphrey

IN A HOUSE on the side of a country meadow, there lived a girl named Yanava. She was a beautiful dark brown child who found it difficult to make things with her hands.

But she thought about many things, and what her hands could not create, her mind could.

Her nearby friends were Oronde, Kengee and Jey. They had played together all their lives, and they had one special thing in common: they all loved Neema, the wise old woman of the town, who had always listened to them and answered their questions.

The children knew that Neema loved colors because of the fine quilts that she made. They also knew that her eyes were growing dim. So they decided they would each give her something that showed their love before the time came when she would not be able to see.

Strategy Tip
Use Pictures to
Get Meaning
Look at the pictures of the characters in this story. What do the pictures show you about Yanava, Oronde, Kengee, Jey, and Neema?

Language Tip
Vocabulary
A quilt is a blanket. It is made of pieces of colored cloth that are sewn together. Her eyes were growing dim means it was getting hard for Neema to see.

Jey looked through the colorful buttons in her old button jar and found some that her grandmother had given her. They were worn with age and all golden on the edges like the setting sun. Jey chose the loveliest buttons of all and strung them on a chain for Neema.

Kengee made ribbon bows from the bits and pieces of bright cloth that she found in her mother's sewing box. She cut and put them together just so, for Kengee cared very much for Neema.

Oronde built a box to hold all of Neema's precious things. He carefully chose each piece of wood. He fitted the pieces together and made a handle so that the box would be easy for Neema to carry. Then he polished the box until it shone with all the love he had put into making it.

While Jey, Kengee and Oronde were working on their gifts, Yanava went to her favorite place to think about what she could give Neema.

Strategy Tip
Understand Character
How do the gifts of Jey, Oronde, and Kengee show how they feel about Neema?

Language Tip
Figurative Language
The author chose the
image of *diamonds* to
tell how much the river
sparkled.

She sat down beside the river which flowed through her yard. "What should the present be?" she asked herself. "Should it be large or small?" And most importantly, "What does Neema need the most?"

It was quiet and peaceful. The river sparkled ever so brightly from the sun. It was as if someone had thrown diamonds upon the water as it flowed by.

Soon the river began to whisper, "Take me into your hands. Take me into your hands." The murmur of the river began to send her into a peaceful sleep.

The river was old and wise with the wisdom of the ancient ones. The river knew the gift that Yanava should give to Neema, the elder.

As Yanava slept, the river murmured over and over, "Take me into your hands. Take me into your hands."

Language Tip
Vocabulary
Murmur means a soft sound that goes on and on. The murmur of the river is the sound of the water flowing by.

Strategy Tip
Stop and Think
Up to this point, the story was realistic, or true to life. What things now happen to let you know that unrealistic and magical things are now happening?

When Yanava awoke it was nighttime, and she knew that the river had given her the answer. She knelt at the water's edge to refresh herself after her nap. As she washed her hands, she began to see rays of light fly off her fingers.

"Can this be?" she said. The harder she rubbed, the brighter the light became.

The river whispered, "You, Yanava, beautiful black child, have the gift of light. Let me show you. Hold out your hands."

She held out her hands, and the light streaming from her fingers changed into different colors.

From her thumbs came the color red, the color of happiness. From her first fingers came the color yellow, the color of the sun which is the soul of all living things. From her second fingers came the color green, the color of life. From her third fingers came the color blue, the color of birth and water. And from her little fingers came the color violet, the color of royalty.

The day finally arrived for the presentation of Neema's gifts.

First to enter the dimly lighted room was Oronde, who presented the box he had made. It was a beautiful box, but Neema could barely see it. "Thank you," she said.

Next came Kengee with her ribbon bows woven together into a colorful piece to hang on the wall. Then came Jey with her old buttons strung on an elegant chain. But it was difficult for Neema to see these gifts in the dim light of the room.

Study Tip
Point of View
This story is told by
someone outside the
story's action. How
would this story be
different if it were being
told by Yanava? How
would it be different if
it were told by Neema?

At last came Yanava, who had waited patiently while the others presented their gifts. She kissed Neema on the forehead and asked politely, "Now may I present my gift?" Neema nodded.

Yanava reached into her bag and took out a jar of river water. Carefully, she removed the lid and poured the water into her hands as the ancient river had told her to do. Then she rubbed her hands together, and the light rays began to form just as they had by the river's edge.

Yanava stood with her hands extended as the colors of the rainbow flowed from her fingers. The dark room was transformed into a vision of color, and Neema could see. *Neema could see!*

Now Neema could see all of her presents because of Yanava's special gift—the gift of light.

Language Tip
Vocabulary
Transformed means completely changed.

Strategy Tip
Understand Plot
Why did Yanava give her gift last? What made her gift the most special gift?

I Asked the Boy
Who Cannot See

Anonymous

I asked the little boy who cannot see,
"And what is colour like?"
"Why, green," said he,
"Is like the rustle of the wind when it blows through
The forest; running water, that is blue;
And red is like a trumpet sound; and pink
Is like the smell of roses; and I think
That purple must be like a thunderstorm;
And yellow is like something soft and warm;
And white is a pleasant stillness when you lie
And dream."

Write About It

Choose one of the colors in the poem. Make a list of things that you think the color is like.

Tell what you learned.

1. Draw a picture to show how a rainbow is created.

2. How does a prism break up light into color?

3. Use paint or make a collage of pictures to express your ideas and feelings about your favorite color.

4. Why is a rainbow important in the story *The River That Gave Gifts?*

5. What is the best gift that you ever gave someone? What is the best gift that you ever received? What made them so special?

The Middle Ages

Tell what you know.

These are pictures from the Middle Ages. What was life like in the Middle Ages?

Word Bank

books

buildings

clothes

farms

furniture

weapons

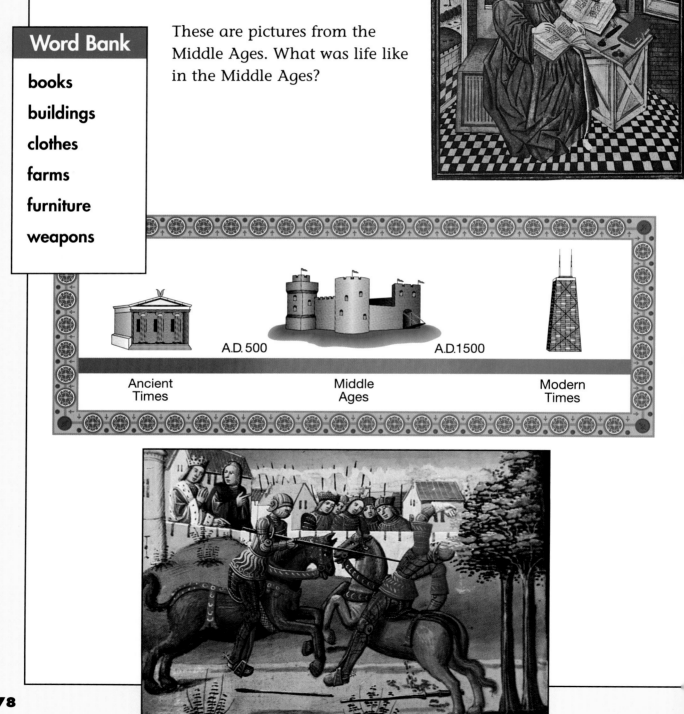

A.D. 500

A.D. 1500

Ancient
Times

Middle
Ages

Modern
Times

Talk About It

How was life in the Middle Ages the same as for people today? How was it different?

Why do you think the Middle Ages got their name?

Life in the Middle Ages

People and Castles

During the Middle Ages in Western Europe, most people lived in small villages. There was no strong government to keep the peace and protect people. As a result, there was a lot of fighting.

There were three groups, or **classes**, in society: fighters, peasants, and clergy.

Lords were fighters. A lord controlled an area of land. A lord's role was to protect the people in that area. Lords often fought other lords to get more land. **Knights** worked for a lord. They fought when their lord ordered them to fight.

Peasants were farmers. They did not own land. They were not free to move from place to place. The lord let peasants live on his land. In return, they gave the lord part of their crops. They did other work for the lord as well.

Clergy were priests. Their role was to teach people about the Christian religion and to pray. Almost no one except the clergy could read and write in the Middle Ages. The clergy helped preserve learning and books during the Middle Ages.

Talk About It

What groups in today's society have roles like the three groups in the Middle Ages? What other groups are there in today's society?

Life in a Castle

Some lords lived in **castles.** Many castles were large stone buildings with thick walls. The castles were designed for defense. The walls kept enemies out.

Castles could supply their own needs. People ate food grown on the lord's land. Servants in the castle made cloth from wool and sewed it into clothes. A well in the castle supplied water.

The stone rooms of the castle were cold and uncomfortable. Often, fireplaces supplied heat during winter, but they could warm only small areas. The great hall was the biggest room in the castle. People ate their meals in the great hall.

The lord had many duties. The lord provided law and justice in the area. He settled quarrels and punished those who did wrong. A **lady** was the lord's wife. She also had many duties. She had to supervise the work of servants who made the meals and sewed clothes. She took care of the sick. When the lord was away fighting, she did many of his duties, too.

Lord's Daily Activities
Eat breakfast (at dawn)
Go to church
Hunt
Fighting practice
Eat dinner (from 10 a.m. to noon)
Hold court to settle quarrels
Take care of his farms and lands
Eat supper
Listen to music and tell stories
Play games such as checkers

Write About It

Write your own daily schedule. Do you like to do the same things every day? How much of your time do you spend on work? How much of your time do you spend on fun?

Knights

Knights needed to learn to become good fighters. It took many years of training for a boy to become a knight.

At the age of seven, a boy went to live with a lord. Often the lord was a relative or a friend of his family. The boy became a **page**. For seven years, pages studied riding, hunting, and good manners. Pages also learned reading, writing, and arithmetic.

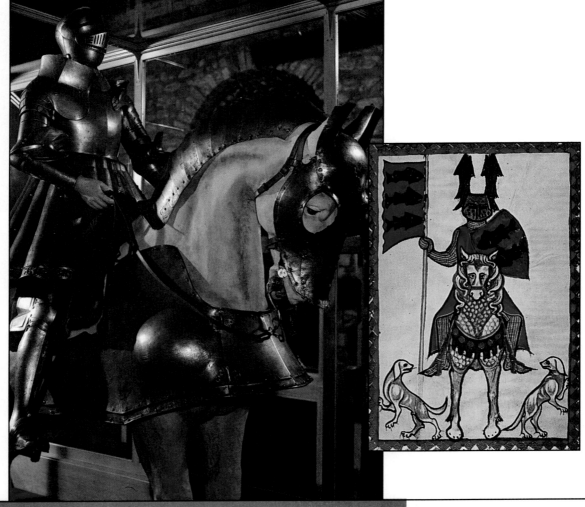

At the age of about fourteen, pages became **squires.** They spent the next seven years learning the art of war. They learned to fight with swords and spears. They learned how to shoot bows and arrows. They learned how to take care of armor. Armor was the iron suit that a knight wore in battle. Sometimes squires went into battle with their knights or lords. The squire's job was to help the lords and take care of their armor.

Playing games such as chess was part of learning good manners.

At the age of about twenty-one, squires became knights. There was a special ceremony. The new knight promised to be brave and to follow the rules of good behavior in war and in peace. He received a sword and spurs.

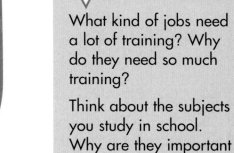

? Think About It

What kind of jobs need a lot of training? Why do they need so much training?

Think about the subjects you study in school. Why are they important for you to learn?

PERCH

CARP

LAMPREY

Food in the Middle Ages

People in the Middle Ages ate many of the same foods you do. They also ate things you may not often eat.

Lords and ladies ate meats such as boar and rabbits. They ate birds such as partridges, swans, larks, and pheasants. A special treat was a fish dish with eels. Dessert might be a cake made in the shape of a castle and filled with fruit, honey, and nuts.

The main meal of the day began around 10 o'clock in the morning and lasted two hours. People ate with spoons and knives and their fingers. They did not have forks. They shared their cups.

▲ People had to wash their hands often during a meal. They poured the water from pitchers like this.

▲ When a peacock was served for dinner, the cook often put the feathers back on.

During the Middle Ages, there was no way to keep food cold. So people used salt to keep food from going bad. People used spices to cover the taste of the salty food.

Peasants did not have as many foods to eat. They usually ate bread. They ate thick soups made from dried beans. They sometimes ate chickens. They rarely ate other meats.

Talk About It

Which foods from the Middle Ages have you eaten? Which foods would you like to taste?

The Last Battle

*Adapted by
Gwen Gross*

Study Tip
Stories about King Arthur are legends. They were first told by people in the Middle Ages. A *legend* is a story that people told for many years before it was written down. Some parts of a legend may be true, but most events never really happened.

Reader's Tip
Arthur's huge Round Table was in the great hall of his castle. It was so big that all his knights could sit down at the same time.

he fame of the Round Table spread far and wide. King Arthur's knights rode through the land. They helped the poor and the weak. Wherever they found evil, they fought against it. Brave men came from many countries to join the Round Table. And gold letters spelled their names upon their chairs.

But the years passed. King Arthur's hair turned silver. His knights, too, grew older. Some died. Some returned to the homes they had left long ago.

Now there were empty places at the Round Table. And no gold letters wrote the names of new knights to come. King Arthur knew the glory of the Round Table was near its end.

Then an evil knight came to Camelot. His name was Sir Mordred. And he was the son of Morgan Le Fay. Mordred pretended to love King Arthur. But like his mother before him, he wanted the throne for himself.

Reader's Tip
Camelot was the place in Arthur's kingdom where his castle and court were.

Reader's Tip
Morgan Le Fay was a character in other stories about King Arthur. She was a wicked magician who was an enemy of King Arthur.

Reader's Tip
Predict
Do you think King
Arthur and Sir Mordred
will make peace? Or do
you think they will fight?
Why?

Language Tip
Vocabulary
To draw a sword is to
pull a sword out of its
holder and get ready to
fight.

*Mordred gathered an army to fight Arthur for the
kingdom. One night Arthur dreamed that Lancelot,
his best knight, was coming to help him. He must
delay the battle with Mordred to give Lancelot time to
arrive. Arthur sent a message saying he would make
Mordred the next king if Mordred would make peace.*

The next morning Arthur and Mordred each set off
to meet together and make the peace. But King Arthur
did not trust Mordred. He told his men, "Be on your
guard. If one sword is drawn, we will fight."

Mordred did not trust King Arthur either. He
warned his men, "If anyone draws a sword, kill
them all."

The two armies were face to face as the sun rose. Arthur and Mordred rode up to each other. Ready to make the peace. Arthur could hardly bear to look at Mordred's proud, evil face. But he wanted peace. For then perhaps the Round Table would not end.

Just then a snake slithered through the grass. It bit one of King Arthur's knights. The knight did not think. He drew his sword. He cut the snake in two.

Strategy Tip
Use Context to
Understand Words
You may not know the
meaning of slithered,
but you can guess from
the sentence that it
tells how a snake moves.

Strategy Tip
Cause and Effect
Which side drew the
first sword? Why? How
did the battle begin?

Mordred's men saw the flash of the sword. And in an instant the battle had begun.

The armies galloped toward each other. Arrows filled the air. Spears crashed against shields. Brave knights fell. Others were wounded. Blood stained the earth. But both sides fought on.

It was almost dark. The battlefield grew quiet. King Arthur looked around him. Of all his knights only two were alive. And they were wounded. Sir Lucan and Sir Bedivere.

Tears ran down King Arthur's face. Just then he saw someone else still standing. Mordred!

"Give me my spear!" Arthur cried. He ran toward his enemy. "You will not do more evil!" he shouted. Mordred saw him. Arthur sank his spear deep into Mordred's heart. But as he died Mordred swung his sword one last time. Arthur fell with a terrible wound.

Strategy Tip
Understand Time Words
The words "It was almost dark" tell you that the battle lasted all day.

Strategy Tip
Understand Plot
At the end of the battle, who is still alive? What happens to Arthur and Mordred?

Language Tip
Idiom
My time has come is a
way of saying that it is
time to die.

Sir Bedivere went to him. Arthur opened his eyes. He pointed to a lake nearby. Then he told Bedivere, "My time has come. Take my magic sword and throw it in the lake. And tell me what you see."

Sir Bedivere took the beautiful sword. But he thought to himself, "How can I throw away the king's sword?" And he hid it under the roots of a tree.

When he came back, King Arthur asked, "Tell me, what did you see?"

Bedivere answered, "Nothing but the moon on the water."

Then Arthur told him, "You have not done what I asked. Go back. And hurry!"

Bedivere went back to the tree. He took the sword in his hand. But still he thought, "I cannot bear to throw my dear king's sword away." So he left it.

Strategy Tip
Understand Plot
What did King Arthur ask Bedivere to do? What did Bedivere do instead?

When he returned, Arthur asked again, "Tell me what you saw."

And Bedivere said, "Nothing but the wind in the trees."

This time King Arthur said, "You have been false to me again! It grows late. My life is leaving me. I can wait no longer. Now, if you care for me, do as I say!"

Then Sir Bedivere was sorry. He found the sword. And he took it to the water's edge. He threw it into the lake as far and as hard as he could.

The sword gleamed in the moonlight. Then a hand rose out of the water. It caught the sword. And disappeared beneath the waves.

Bedivere told King Arthur what he had seen. Arthur nodded. "Now help me to the water's edge. And hurry. I have so little time. I am afraid I have waited too long."

Strategy Tip
Draw Conclusions
How does King Arthur know that Bedivere has kept his promise?

Reader's Tip
King Arthur's sword was a magic sword. In the legend, the young Arthur had pulled the sword out of a stone. No one else could get the sword out. Arthur became king because he was able to pull it out.

When they reached the shore, a boat was there. Three women were in it. They wore crowns and long black veils. When they saw King Arthur, they began to cry softly.

"Put me in the boat," Arthur said. Sir Bedivere set him down gently. One of the women cried, "Oh, Arthur! Why did you wait so long? Your wound has grown cold."

The boat sailed slowly into the mist. Sir Bedivere called out, "My king! Will you return?"

King Arthur answered, "I am going to a magic land. There I will be healed. Unless it is too late. But if England has need of me, I will come again." And the boat disappeared in the mist.

Some say King Arthur died. Some say he is sleeping an enchanted sleep. Some say he lives on in a land of mists and magic. And that one day he will return. And there will be a new kingdom of the good and the true.

Strategy Tip
Draw Conclusions
Do you think King Arthur died? Why or why not?

Make a coat of arms.

Knights in the Middle Ages had coats of arms. A knight's coat of arms showed who the knight was. That way he could be recognized as a friend or enemy in battle. Many coats of arms had pictures of flowers and animals.

Make your own coat of arms.

1. Get heavy paper and markers, crayons, or paints.

2. Draw a shape like the one in the pictures. Cut out the shape.

3. Think of things that tell about you or your family. They can show what you like to do or what jobs members of your family have. Draw them on the cut out paper.

4. Tell a friend about your coat of arms.

Tell what you learned.

1. Who were the three main groups in society in the Middle Ages? What role did each have?

2. Why were knights important in the society of the Middle Ages? Explain how someone became a knight.

3. What did you learn about the role of knights from the story "The Last Battle"?

4. Legends are often based on facts. What parts of the story of King Arthur do you think might have been true? What parts of the story are not true?

Trade in the Middle Ages

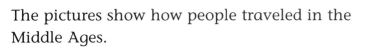

Tell what you know.

The pictures show how people traveled in the Middle Ages.

What can you tell about how people traveled? How was it different from the way people travel today?

Talk About It

Have you ever traveled to another country for a visit? What did you learn from your travels?

How do faster ways to travel make it easier to learn about other countries and customs?

103

The Growth of Towns

During the late Middle Ages in Western Europe, towns began to get bigger, and new towns appeared. Why was this possible?

Historians think this growth began on the farms. Inventions made it easier for peasants to plow fields, so they grew more crops. The extra food could feed people in cities.

During the same period, lords wanted to buy goods, such as cloth, weapons, and spices. **Merchants** started businesses in towns to sell these goods. Where merchants settled, others followed. Towns grew larger.

▲ When people invented better plows like this one, they could grow more food.

◀ As towns grew, shops appeared.

▲ Glassblowers

By the 1300s, Europe had many towns. Most had fewer than 10,000 people. People in towns lived by exchanging goods and services. They no longer produced all their own food and clothing, as people in villages and castles did.

Towns began to have teachers, lawyers, shopkeepers, and bankers. This new group of people, the **middle class**, slowly grew in numbers. Towns grew into cities. Cities and the middle class became important in modern times in Western Europe.

▲ Butchers

◀ Carpenter

Word Bank

banks

businesses

money

shops

trade

Think About It

What makes the city different from the country?

What is needed for cities to grow?

Trade in the Middle Ages

Trade also took place over long distances. Europeans **imported** more and more things they wanted from other countries. Europeans wanted to buy goods from Asia and other distant places. They wanted spices such as pepper, cinnamon, and ginger. They wanted rich cloth such as silk, cotton, and damask from the East. They wanted perfumes and medicines.

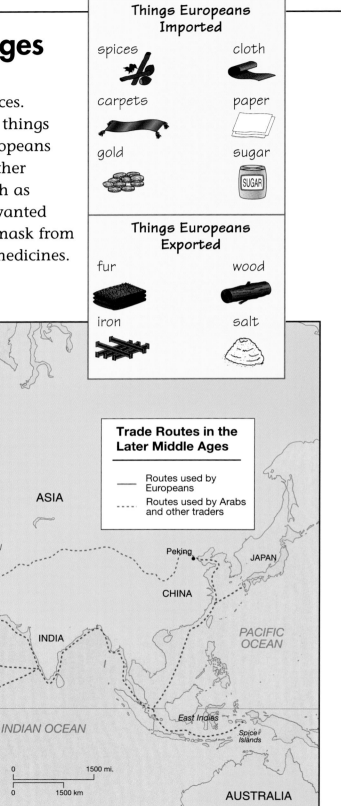

Things Europeans Imported

spices   cloth

carpets   paper

gold   sugar

Things Europeans Exported

fur   wood

iron   salt

Trade Routes in the Later Middle Ages

——— Routes used by Europeans

- - - Routes used by Arabs and other traders

ENGLAND
London
Paris
FRANCE
EUROPE
Venice
ITALY
SPAIN
BLACK SEA
CASPIAN SEA
ASIA
MEDITERRANEAN SEA
Baghdad
ISLAMIC COUNTRIES
RED SEA
Mecca
AFRICA
INDIA
Peking
CHINA
JAPAN
PACIFIC OCEAN
Equator
INDIAN OCEAN
East Indies
Spice Islands
ATLANTIC OCEAN
AUSTRALIA

0   1500 mi.
0   1500 km

Europeans began to trade more and more with Arab traders. Arab peoples controlled many sea routes. These routes led to countries that were farther to the east, such as India and China.

Europeans learned many things from the Arab world. Europeans adapted the way Arabs wrote numbers. They learned about medicines. They learned better ways to navigate ships. Arabs had an invention that measured the position of the sun and stars. By using the invention, sailors could always know where they were.

Try It Out

Today there is much international trade. Many products have labels telling where they were imported from. Look at the labels on your clothing and things you have with you at school. What countries are the things from? Locate the countries on a world map.

Marco Polo

Marco Polo, a merchant from Italy, was the most famous traveler of the Middle Ages. He was the son of a merchant who traded in jewels. In 1271, at the age of 17, Marco Polo went with his father on a trip to China. They traveled east from Italy by ship to Asia. They traveled across Asia by camel and foot. Marco arrived in China four years later, when he was 21 years old. Few Europeans had ever traveled that far.

Marco Polo stayed in China for seventeen years. He met the powerful ruler of China, the Great Khan, and worked for him.

Marco Polo was amazed by the things he saw in China. He saw the Khan's great palace with rooms of gold and silver. He saw people dressed in rich silks. He saw people using paper money. He had never seen such things before.

When Marco Polo went back to Europe, he wrote a book about China. People in Europe thought that Polo's stories about China were strange and wonderful. Many did not believe that they were true. People in Europe had never seen things like the things Polo described.

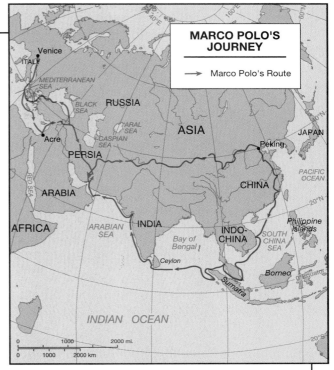

MARCO POLO'S JOURNEY

→ Marco Polo's Route

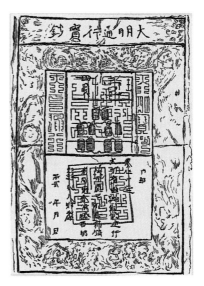

▲ Chinese paper money

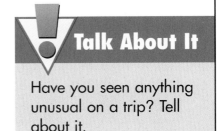

Talk About It

Have you seen anything unusual on a trip? Tell about it.

The Black Death

Europe had one import from the East that it didn't want. The ships that brought so many trade goods to Europe also brought sicknesses no one had seen before. There was often no cure for **disease**, or sickness, in the Middle Ages. No one knew what caused disease. There was no way to stop a disease from spreading to many people.

▼ People everywhere were very afraid because no one knew what caused the Black Death.

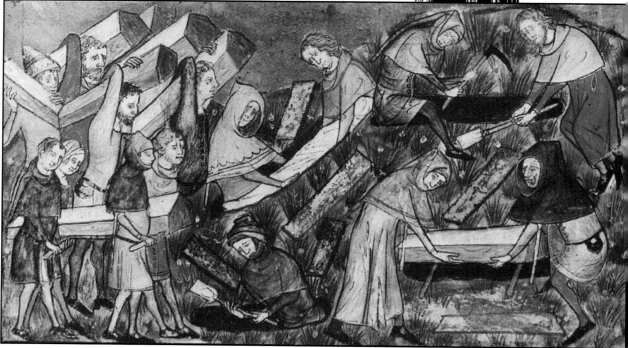

A terrible disease called the Black Death killed many people in Western Europe in the 1300s. Some historians think that one third of the population of Western Europe died of the Black Death. When people caught the disease, they got big sores over their bodies and then smaller black sores. Most people who got the disease died in less than a week.

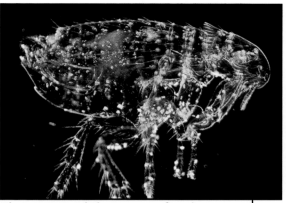

Fleas carried the germs for the disease in their bodies.

Today scientists know that rats carried the disease that caused the Black Death. The rats reached Europe on ships. Fleas bit the rats. The fleas bit people and carried the disease to them. People then spread the disease to other people by coughing.

Doctors did their best to help sick people.

Talk About It

How did the Black Death spread through Europe?

This picture of the ▶ court of the Great Khan was painted around the time that Marco Polo arrived.

From the Story of Marco Polo's Travels

This reading is from the book Marco Polo wrote about his travels in China. He was amazed at the great civilization he found there. Here is Polo's description of a celebration at the court of the Great Khan.

It is true that the people celebrate their New Year's Feast in the month of February. The Great Khan and his people celebrate the feast in this way. It is the custom for the Great Khan and his people, both men and women, to wear white for the feast. They do this because they think white is a lucky color. They start the year wearing white because they want the rest of the year to bring them good things and happiness.

On New Year's Day, the people that the Khan rules bring him fabulous gifts of gold, silver, pearls and other things. Most of the presents are white in color. They do this so that during the year everyone will have wealth, joy, and happiness. On this day, more than ten thousand beautiful and richly decorated horses are given to the Great Khan. And there are more than five hundred elephants all covered with silk and gold. Each elephant carries a box full of gold and silver dishes and other things that are necessary for the feast. All pass in front of the Khan. This is the most wonderful sight that can be seen.

Talk About It

What ideas about the court of the Great Khan do you get from this reading?

What do people from your culture do to celebrate the New Year?

On the Road Again

by Willie Nelson

On the road again.
Just can't wait to get on the road again.
The life I love is making music with my friends,
and I can't wait to get on the road again.

On the road again,
going places that I've never been,
seeing things that I may never see again,
and I can't wait to get on the road again.

Tell what you learned.

1. Why did towns grow during the Middle Ages? What could you see in a town during the Middle Ages?

2. What contacts did Europeans have with other parts of the world during the Middle Ages?

3. There are many pictures in this unit of the Middle Ages. Which picture do you think tells the most about what life was like?

Telling Stories

Word Bank

- **cartoon**
- **letter**
- **magazine**
- **newspaper**
- **novel**
- **textbook**

Tell what you know.

What do you read?
Why do you read?

Tuesday 24th

Dear Alana,

I want to tell you all about what happened to me yesterday. My brother Joaquín and I went to see the eye doctor, the way we do every year. When the doctor checked my eyes, she said I would need glasses! I felt funny about it for a minute, but then I got to pick out the glasses myself. They are red, and I don't even have to wear them all the time. I really like them. I'll show them to you when I see you at New Year.

See you soon,

NEW MOUNTAIN BIKES

Want to buy a new bike and head for some stump-jumping fun? Your adventures may start long before you hit those craggy trails — the huge range in price tags could be the first thing to throw you. The bikes we tested run from dirt cheap (less than $150) to staggeringly steep (more than $700). There's an equally wide range in quality. So how do you get the best bike for your bucks? Remember these rules of the road: The less the bike weighs, the easier it is to pedal. Better gearing helps you climb up hills and race down them. And brakes that take just a short distance to stop improve your chances of avoiding crashes and living to brag about your exploits. We tested 19 bikes for all this and more.

The two cheapest bikes we tested were no bargain: The Huffy *Blades* and the Murray *Eagle River* flunked! Get the facts on …

CHEAP BIKES

Riding these bikes was more work than fun for our testers. First, the two cheapies weighed as much as 10 pounds more than the other bikes in our test. And the gears didn't give our testers much help lugging all that weight uphill. Even though the bikes had 18 speeds, neither bike had low enough gears for steep climbs. (See *Guide to the Gears* below.) In fact, the *Eagle River* had the smallest gear range of all the bikes we tested.

Our testers didn't have to pedal and pant so hard on level ground — which gave them a chance to notice other problems. Gears on both bikes shifted roughly. But that was nothing compared to the rough ride our testers' rumps took once they headed off pavement and onto rocky trails. The bikes didn't absorb those off-road bumps and crags very well. But the testers didn't face their biggest problem until they were

Steer clear: The $130 Murray and Huffy *Blades* (left) were down

ready to stop. Nothing short of a hard squeeze would bring these bikes to a halt. And even that didn't help if the bikes were wet. When the wheels were wet, these bikes took four to five car lengths

GUIDE TO

DE TO GEARS…

turns the front chain turns the chain, which rear wheels go around

"Life, yes — but as for intelligent life, I have my doubts."

Gloria Whelan

Goodbye, Vietnam

Share an
unforgettable
journey...

A Bullseye Book

om House 0-679-82376-X $3.99 U.S. / $4.99 CAN.

Incas

ans

📖 READING

Prereading

Look at the picture. Do you know about this place? Where is it?

Hiram Bingham and the Lost City of Machu Picchu

Hiram Bingham (1875–1956) was a history teacher. He
wanted to learn about the ancient people of South America.
He visited South America five times and discovered many
ancient ruins. His most famous discovery was in Peru. It was
5 the ruins of Machu Picchu, the lost city of the Incas.

The Incas lived in South America for three hundred years.
Then, in the 1500s, they lost a war with the Spanish. The
Spanish tried to destroy everything that the Incas built, but
people said there was still an old city somewhere in the
10 mountains.

Many people searched for Machu Picchu, but no one found
it. Then, in 1911, Bingham learned about some ruins on a
mountain next to the Urubamba River. Bingham climbed the
mountain, and there was the city!
15 At one time, a thousand people lived in Machu Picc
They built long streets and beautiful stone buildi
building was an observatory where they watche
moon, and stars. They told time by the stars an
calendar to mark the hours, days, and years.
20 When did these people leave Machu Picc
they go? No one knows.

Today tourists can take buses up to the
They walk on the streets and take pictures
like being in this ancient place.

Meaning fr

destroy: make into ruins

still: at that time

learned what time

◥ Talk About It

How many ways did
you use reading today?

PHOTOGRAPHER—KEN LAX

ILLUSTRATOR—KEN TEN

150
n.

nd as

7. _____

8. _____

Reading Stories

What kind of story is it?

Stories are fun. You see stories in newspapers, magazines, books, movies, and television. Stories are one way people share news and ideas.

Nonfiction stories are about real people, places, or events. Nonfiction authors write about things that really happened. Books about history are nonfiction. So are newspaper stories.

Fiction stories are imaginary. They are made up by the story's author. The author writes about things that did not really happen.

Try It Out

Tell a fiction story that you like to a partner. Have your partner tell the story to another pair of students.

The people, animals, or imaginary beings in fiction stories are its **characters.** A character is whoever speaks and acts in a story.

The **setting** of a fiction story is where or when the story takes place. The story's setting might be in an imaginary country, in a real place, or in the far future.

The things that happen in the story are the **plot.** When you talk about what movie characters did, or what happened to them, you are talking about the movie's plot.

When a story's characters have problems to solve, the problems are the story's **conflict**. Often the conflicts are solved near the end of the story.

▲ Characters

▲ Setting

▲ Plot

Think About It

Think back on stories you have read so far in this book. Who were the characters? Where were the stories' settings? What happened in the plots?

Choosing a Book

There are many different kinds of fiction and nonfiction stories. Here are some kinds of stories. Which ones would you choose?

Biography is nonfiction about real people's lives. Biography tells where the person was born and what he or she did in life. When someone writes the story of his or her own life, it is called **autobiography.**

▲ This biography tells the life story of Roberto Clemente, a hero in baseball and in life.

Realistic fiction stories could have happened, but did not. The stories are imaginary, but they are set in real places and times. All characters in realistic fiction are human beings.

In this realistic fiction story, Rudy ▶ Herrera is invited to his first pool party. Rudy's friends and family tell him different things about how to behave. Will Rudy have a good time?

In a **mystery,** strange things happen! Perhaps odd noises are coming from an old house, or someone finds a treasure map. The characters in a mystery try to find out what makes the mysterious things happen.

In this mystery story, ▶ young detective Henry Coffin finds the missing mother of a schoolmate.

History is nonfiction about things that happened in the past. A book about real events in the Middle Ages is a history book.

▲ This history tells what immigration to the United States is like. The book's photographs show immigrants in the 1800s and today.

Talk About It

What books of these kinds have you read? Which kinds of books did you like best? Why?

What makes a story a fantasy?

In **fantasy fiction,** things happen that are impossible in real life. Many television stories are fantasies. Many cartoons and comic books are fantasies.

The things that make a story a fantasy might be the characters, setting, or plot.

A fantasy story's setting might be imaginary. It might be a city under the sea or a magic forest.

Impossible things may happen in the plot. A person may become an animal, or a machine might act like a human being.

Fantasy characters might have special powers. They may be able to fly or read minds.

Here is an example of fantasy.

The Horse had lifted its head. Shasta stroked its smooth-as-satin nose and said, "I wish *you* could talk, old fellow."

And then for a second he thought he was dreaming, for quite distinctly, though in a low voice, the Horse said, "But I can."

Shasta stared into its great eyes and his own grew almost as big, with astonishment.

"However did *you* learn to talk?" he asked.

"Hush! Not so loud," replied the Horse. "Where I come from, nearly all the animals talk."

"Wherever is that?" asked Shasta.

"Narnia," answered the Horse.

The Horse and His Boy by C. S. Lewis.

Talk About It

What things in this passage make this story a fantasy?

What other fantasy stories do you know? Tell about them.

How Scientists Work

Scientists carefully test their ideas to make sure they are true. This careful testing is called **research.** They use the **scientific method** to organize their research.

You can use the scientific method to perform your own experiments.

Scientific Method

1. **Make observations.** You notice that your black sweater seems warmer than your white one on a cold day.

2. **Ask a question.** You ask, "Do black things absorb, or soak up, more heat from sunlight than white things do?"

3. State a hypothesis. A hypothesis is an idea that has yet to be proved true. Your hypothesis might be "Black things absorb more heat than white ones."

4. Test your hypothesis. Invent an experiment to test your hypothesis. Repeat the experiment to make sure of your results.

5. Collect and report data. The observations you write down during your experiment are your data. See the chart on this page.

Is your hypothesis true?

My Record

Time	Black can	White can
1 min.		
2 min.		
3 min.		
4 min.		
5 min.		

Think About It

How are the students testing their hypothesis that black things absorb more heat than white things?

Can you give an example of an idea you can test with the scientific method?

Hey, Al

*Story by
Arthur Yorinks*

*Pictures by
Richard Egielski*

AL, a nice man, a quiet man, a janitor, lived in one room on the West Side with his faithful dog, Eddie. They ate together. They worked together. They watched TV together. What could be bad?

Plenty.

"Look at this dump!" Eddie growled. "We can't have a house? A little back yard to run around in for a change?"

"Oh, sure," Al snapped. "Today it's a house you want. Tomorrow, who knows? Maybe the moon!"

"The moon? *The moon?*" Eddie howled. "Pigeons live better than us!"

No, life wasn't easy for Al and Eddie. They were always working, always struggling. It was always something.

Strategy Tip
Understand Character
What can you tell about Eddie and Al from their dialogue?

Strategy Tip
Stop and Think
When did you know this
story was a fantasy?

One morning, while Al was shaving, a voice called to him. "Hey, Al," it said. Al turned and saw a bird. A large bird.

"Al," said the bird, "are you working too hard? Still struggling and going nowhere? *Hmmm?* Listen. Have I got a place for you. No worries, no cares—it's terrific."

"Huh?" Al said. He was confused.

"Al, Al, *Al!* You need a change. Tomorrow, come and be my guest. Eddie, too. You'll see, you'll *love* it!"

Then, with a few flaps, the bird was gone.

You can imagine that evening's conversation. Eddie was already packing.

"*What?* Just quit my job?" Al said.

"There's more to life than mops and pails!" Eddie insisted.

"But—"

"That's it, we're going. I don't want to hear another word."

At dawn, they were both in the bathroom. Waiting.

The large bird appeared, and Al and Eddie were ferried thousands of feet upward to an island in the sky.

Strategy Tip
Stop and Think
Why were Al and Eddie waiting?

Language Tip
Vocabulary
Ferried means "carried." The large bird carried Eddie and Al to the island.

Language Tip
Vocabulary
To and fro means back
and forth.

Unbelievable! Lush trees, rolling hills,
gorgeous grass. Birds flitted to and fro. Waterfalls
cascaded into shimmering pools.

"Would you look at this view!" Eddie said.
"WOW!" said Al.

Strategy Tip
Understand Setting
The island in the sky is a fantasy setting. Why?

Birds sang and brought them food. They ate. They drank. They swam. They sunbathed. They never had it so good.

"So, Al, is this so terrible?" the large bird asked.

"What a life," Al cooed. "A guy could live like this forever."

The days passed blissfully. As memories of their old life slowly faded, Al and Eddie decided that this was ecstasy.

But ripe fruit soon spoils.

One morning Al woke up and shrieked. "Eddie! Look at us! We're turning into birds!"

Indeed. Their eyes were a little beady, their noses a bit beak-like.

"We've got to get out of here," he croaked. Wings sprouted. Tail feathers plumed.

"Take us back, take us back!" Eddie quacked. "I don't want to be a bird!"

"*I'd rather mop floors!*" he honked as they both flapped furiously and rose into the air.

Strategy Tip
Stop and Think
What happened to
Eddie? What do you
predict will happen now?

"Eddie, be careful, follow me," Al squawked. But Eddie, in a frenzy, was flying in circles, higher and higher.

Exhausted, straining to stay aloft, he plunged into the open sea and was gone.

Al barely made it home in one piece. Alone, without his friend, he was heartbroken.

But, fortunately, Eddie was a talented swimmer, and in no time he found his way back to the West Side.

"Eddie!" Al cried.

"Oh, Al . . ."

Paradise lost is sometimes Heaven found.

Strategy Tip
Use Pictures to Get Meaning
How have Al and Eddie changed at the end of the story? How does the picture tell you that they have changed?

Language Tip
Vocabulary
Paradise is another word for heaven.

Study Tips
Story Impressions
As soon as you finish the story, write down your feelings about *Hey, Al.* Did you like the story? Why or why not? Which things in the story did you like or dislike?

Home, Sweet Home

'Mid pleasures and palaces though we may roam,
Be it ever so humble, there's no place like home.

A charm from the skies seems to hallow us there,
Which seek through the world is ne'er met with elsewhere.

Home! Home! Sweet, sweet home!
Be it ever so humble, there's no place like home.

Think About It

How does this song
relate to the story
Hey, Al?

Tell what you learned.

1. What is the difference between fiction and nonfiction stories?

2. What is your favorite fiction book? Make a chart about it.

Name of Book	
Setting	
Characters	
Plot	

3. What makes *Hey, Al* a fantasy story?

4. How would you change the plot of *Hey, Al* so that Eddie and Al got the yard they wanted in the beginning of the story? Decide if you will make your story a fantasy or not.

CHAPTER 7

Writing Stories

Tell what you know.

Spoken languages sound different from one another. Written languages look different from one another.

Do you recognize any of these languages? Can you read the signs?

▲ Italian

▲ Swahili

German ▶

▲ Russian

▼ Chinese

INTERDIT
DE 0ʰ A 16ʰ 00
LES MARDI, JEUDI, SAMEDI
SAUF AUX VÉHICULES
DES COMMERÇANTS DU MARCHE

▲ French

pza. de la
Independencia ⬆

← P Recoletos

← P Colón

←   museo
     Arqueológico

▲ Spanish

Talk About It

How many languages can you speak or write?

How is learning a new language a challenge?

141

Different Ways of Writing

When you write in English, you are using an alphabet with 26 letters. The alphabet used in English is a Roman alphabet. The letters come from the alphabet used by the ancient Romans two thousand years ago.

Many other languages use Roman alphabets. Some of them are French, Spanish, Italian, and Portuguese.

In alphabets, letters represent, or stand for, sounds. Letters are symbols for sounds.

▲ The ancient Romans wrote in the Latin language.

Spelling of English Sounds	
Sound	**Spelling and Examples**
d	**did**, fille**d**, a**dd**
l	**l**and, tel**l**

Words for School

French: l'école
Spanish: la escuela
Italian: la scuola
Portuguese: a escola

Roman

Cyrillic

ق
ص

Arabic

ך
ל
שׁ

Hebrew

ア
サ
タ
カ

Japanese

人 person
雨 rain

Chinese

There are many alphabets in addition to the Roman alphabet. Russian uses the Cyrillic alphabet. Arabic uses the Arabic alphabet. Hebrew uses the Hebrew alphabet.

One way of writing Japanese is with symbols that stand for syllables. Syllables are word parts, not single sounds. There are forty-six basic syllables in Japanese. The symbols above are part of a Japanese syllabary.

The Chinese language doesn't use an alphabet. It is written with symbols that developed from picture writing. Symbols stand for whole words. Some symbols look a little like the things they stand for.

Write About It

Write a message to a partner in pictures. Then write it in your native language and in English. Is the message different when the message is written in a different way? Which message was the hardest for you to write?

A Treasury of Words

Dictionaries list words. Dictionaries in English are in **alphabetical order**. Words that begin with *a* come first, then words that begin with *b*, and so on.

You can get a lot of information about words in a dictionary. Dictionaries tell how to say words. They give **pronunciations** of words. Dictionaries tell what words mean. They give **definitions** of words. Often dictionaries give sentences that show how to use the word. These are called **context sentences**.

Words in English come from many different languages. Many dictionaries tell you which language the word comes from.

Some dictionaries have pictures to help you understand word meaning.

Here are some dictionary **entries.**

entry   pronunciation   definition   word origin

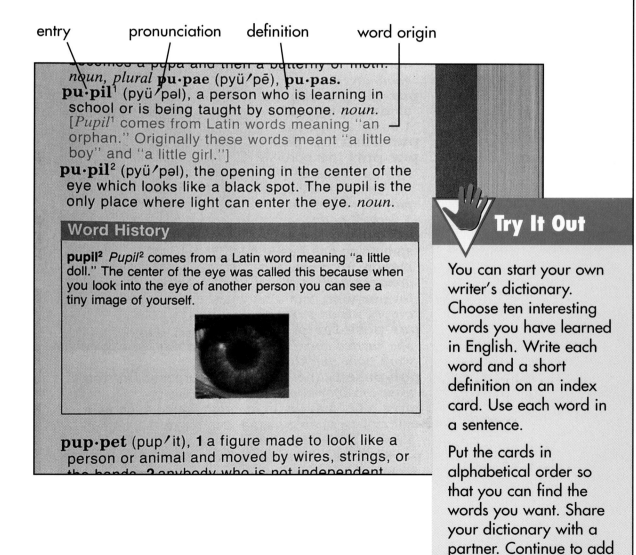

~~becomes a pupa and then a butterfly or moth.~~
noun, plural **pu·pae** (pyü′pē), **pu·pas.**
pu·pil¹ (pyü′pəl), a person who is learning in school or is being taught by someone. *noun.* [*Pupil¹* comes from Latin words meaning "an orphan." Originally these words meant "a little boy" and "a little girl."]
pu·pil² (pyü′pəl), the opening in the center of the eye which looks like a black spot. The pupil is the only place where light can enter the eye. *noun.*

Word History

pupil² *Pupil²* comes from a Latin word meaning "a little doll." The center of the eye was called this because when you look into the eye of another person you can see a tiny image of yourself.

pup·pet (pup′it), **1** a figure made to look like a person or animal and moved by wires, strings, or ~~the hands. 2 anybody who is not independent.~~

Try It Out

You can start your own writer's dictionary. Choose ten interesting words you have learned in English. Write each word and a short definition on an index card. Use each word in a sentence.

Put the cards in alphabetical order so that you can find the words you want. Share your dictionary with a partner. Continue to add to your card dictionary.

How do you use writing?

You write in many ways every day. You write in school to learn. You also write to share your ideas and feelings.

Is writing important to you? In what ways do you use writing? Have you written things like these?

Book Report

<u>**Title:**</u> The Pool Party

<u>**Author:**</u> Gary Soto

<u>**Summary:**</u> A boy named Rudy Herrera is excited when he gets an invitation to go to a pool party from the most popular girl in school. The problem is he has never been to a pool party before. His family gives him advice on how to act. He goes to the party with a huge inner tube, makes friends, and has a great time.

<u>**Why**</u> <u>**I**</u> <u>**liked**</u> <u>**the**</u> <u>**book:**</u> I liked reading about the huge inner tube and the party.

My Lab Report

Hypothesis: Black things absorb more heat than white ones.

Method: I used two jars. I covered one with white paper and the other with black paper. I used a lamp for heat. I put a thermometer on each jar to measure changes in temperature.

VOLUME XXIX
BULLETIN

Word Bank

book reports

fiction stories

journal

letters

newspaper articles

poems

recipes

Delicious Day!

The seventh-grade class had an international snack day last Thursday. Students and their families made snacks from all over the world. During lunch, students from the entire school had the chance to taste the treats. Foods included salsa from Mexico, hummus from the Middle East, and pierogi from Poland. "Everything tasted great!" said Marta Guerrero, from eighth grade. "And I even got a great new recipe for salsa."

Monday, September 25

Today at school, Ms. Coutré asked me to lead the dance class! I showed the class some new steps that I learned at my old school.

The Old Castle

The castle looked old and weary. Its walls leaned against each other, as if it would collapse in a minute or so. They looked around the castle. At the back, they found an old door. It looked as if it hadn't been used for years. The door looked as if it would be possible to open. The boys stood there, trying to make a decision.

Talk About It

Is writing important to you? What kinds of writing do you usually do?

Who writes?

Many people use writing in their jobs. For example, people in offices must write letters and memos to communicate their ideas.

Some people have jobs in which they do a lot of writing. Here are a few of these jobs.

When you read a story in the newspaper, you are reading the work of a **journalist.** Journalists must get the facts about what happens and why. They interview people and ask questions. They ask about when and where something happened and who was there. Then journalists write the answers to these questions in their stories.

Talk About It

Do any of the jobs described interest you? Why or why not?

When you read directions for a computer game, you are reading the work of a **technical writer.** Technical writers have to get the right information on how things work. They use computer programs themselves so that they can write about them. They must write clearly and simply.

When you read a book in your native language by an author from the United States, you are reading the work of a **translator.** Translators need to know two languages very well. They have to understand what the author of a book is trying to say. Then they can write the same ideas in another language.

▲ Laura Dail translates books from Spanish into English.

Try It Out

Find a poem or a story written in your native language. Translate all or part of it into English for your classmates to read.

Write about yourself.

This is a story written by a student about the first day at a new school.

The First Day

When I first entered Al-Banyan School, I started shivering and my heart was beating so fast. I wondered, "How would this school be? Would my classmates be kind and friendly like my old friends?" In my classroom, everything seemed strange to me. I looked at the boys and girls sitting around me and imagined them as monsters and aliens. They stared at me. I tried to ignore them and pretend to be normal.

At recess time, a girl from our class came to me and asked me about my name. We talked and laughed together. She told me a little about herself, and I told her a little about my school in Dubai. After a few days, I felt much better. I had plenty of friends, and my teachers helped me study and catch up with the rest of the class. Now I like my new school very much, and I wish I could stay here forever.

Bedoor Al-Shebli, Age 11
Banyan Bilingual School, Kuwait

Jong Bum (James) Song

Sunnyside N.Y 11104

"How My Family Decided To Move To The Place We Are Now"

My family decided to move to the place we are now because my father had come here alone and my family missed him. My family also decided to come here for a better education

Hi. My name's Lara. I'm a Spanish girl. I live in Gijón. It's a big city in the North of Spain. I'm 12 years old. I've got long brown hair and green eyes. I'm medium height.
I'm a student. My mother has a book shop.

My name is Jessica Gamboa Garza

I'm from Reynosa Tamaulipas, Mexico.
I was born on October 10.
I'm 13 years old.

Write About It

Write about an interesting event in your life. What happened? Why is the event important to you?

Blame

by Shel Silverstein

I wrote such a beautiful book for you
'Bout rainbows and sunshine
And dreams that come true.
But the goat went and ate it
(You knew that he would),
So I wrote you another one
Fast as I could.
Of course it could never be
Nearly as great
As that beautiful book
That the silly goat ate.
So if you don't like
This new book I just wrote—
Blame the goat.

Tell what you learned.

1. Imagine you are a teacher. Describe for your class how to use a dictionary.

2. What kind of writing did you do during the last week? List your reasons for writing.

3. Write a short book report about one of the stories you have read so far in this book.

Book Report
Title: The Pool Party
Author: Gary Soto
Summary: A boy named Rudy Herrera is excited when he gets an invitation to go to a pool party from the most popular girl in school. The problem is he has never been to a pool party before. His family gives him advice on how to act. He goes to the party with a huge inner tube, makes friends, and has a great time.
Why I liked the book: I liked reading about the huge inner tube and the party.

Mysteries

Tell what you know.

Word Bank

art

defense

fun

politics

religion

These things were made by people long ago. What are they? What do you think they were used for?

What do these things tell about the people who made them?

Mysteries in History

Who were the Inca?

In the 1400s, a huge empire was created in South America. It is called the Inca empire. The Inca developed an amazing **civilization.** The Inca were great builders. They built stone cities and roads. The empire had more than 10,000 miles (16,000 kilometers) of roads. Some parts of the roads still exist. Inca crafts workers made beautiful things from gold and silver. Weavers made fine cloth. Doctors performed brain surgery.

However, the Inca did not have a written language. They did not know about the wheel. How then did the huge empire function? It was held together by a strong government and a good system of communication. A king headed the government. Speedy runners carried the king's orders throughout the empire.

Workers had specific duties. Some people grew corn or raised animals. Some people made pottery. People gave part of what they made to the government. It then distributed the goods.

? Think About It

Why would it be hard to build roads and cities without the wheel?

Look at the map of the Inca empire. Parts of what present-day nations made up the Inca empire?

The End of the Inca Empire

In 1532, the Inca empire was defeated by the Spanish. More than 12 million Inca were defeated by fewer than 200 Spanish soldiers. How could this happen?

In 1527, the Inca ruler Huayna Capac died. A **civil war** soon broke out. Two of his sons, Huáscar and Atahualpa, and their followers fought each other. The civil war did not end until 1532. Huáscar was dead, and Atahualpa's army was greatly weakened.

▲ Huayna Capac

▲ Atahualpa meeting with a Spaniard.

Just at that time, Francisco Pizarro arrived. He was a Spanish explorer who had heard rumors of a rich empire in South America. In a surprise attack, Pizarro defeated Atahualpa's army. The Spanish had guns and horses, which were unknown to the Inca. Pizarro captured Atahualpa and demanded gold and silver for his release. The gold and silver were paid, but Pizarro killed Atahualpa anyway. Without a king to lead them, the Inca empire fell apart. The Spanish took control.

◀ Francisco Pizarro

Write About It

What technology did the Spanish have that the Inca did not?

A civil war is a war among the people within a country. How is a civil war different from other wars?

The Mystery of Machu Picchu

The Spanish wanted complete control of the Inca empire. But they didn't know about Machu Picchu, a city high in the Andes Mountains. For hundreds of years, it sat abandoned. Only a few people in the area knew it was there. But in 1911, an archaeologist from the United States named Hiram Bingham saw the city. Then people around the world learned of this beautiful and mysterious place.

▲ Indians from Peru showed Hiram Bingham where Machu Picchu was.

▲ The Inca people built everything at Machu Picchu by hand.

The city seemed almost the same as when the last Inca had left. But when and why did they leave? And when exactly was the city built? These and other questions may never be answered. Some people think Inca nobles hid there after the Spanish took control. Since the Inca left no written records, it is difficult to know for sure. More than 200 stone structures remain. These include houses, staircases, temples, and water tanks. Today, Machu Picchu is one of the most famous historical sites in the world.

Talk About It

Study the picture of Machu Picchu. What words can you use to describe the city?

Machu Picchu is a famous historical site in Peru. What is a famous historical site in the country where you and your family come from? What historic places have you visited? What places would you like to visit?

The Andes

Machu Picchu is in the Andes Mountains. The Andes are the longest chain of mountains in the world. They are about 4,500 miles (7,240 kilometers) long. Several of the Andes Mountains are more than 20,000 feet (6,100 meters) high.

Some of the Andes are so high that they have **glaciers,** or huge masses of ice, on them. A few of the mountains are volcanoes. They sometimes erupt and blow out steam, ashes, and melted rock.

▲ These terraced fields look like giant stairs.

Since before the time of the Incas, people in the Andes have been farmers and herders. Farmers build terraces in the steep mountain to raise crops. They bring water to the crops with irrigation systems. Farmers grow grains such as corn, potatoes, and quinoa, which is a grain native to the area. Higher up the mountains, where the climate is too cold to grow crops, people raise sheep and cattle. They also raise two animals that are native to the Andes, llamas and alpacas.

Word Bank

cold

green

high

mountainous

rocky

? Think About It

Have you ever been in the mountains? What was the area like?

Plan a visit to a glacier. What kind of clothes would you need?

The Nazcas' Secret

by Carol Anderson

Reader's Tip

The Nazca people lived in Peru two thousand years ago. That was more than a thousand years before the Inca people. There are still many mysteries about the Nazca people. This story tells about some of those mysteries.

Language Tip
Vocabulary

A *condor* is a large bird like an eagle. *Triangles* and *rectangles* are shapes with three and four sides. A *zigzag* is a wiggly line. A *spiral* is a line that curves around itself in a circle. A *crown* is worn on the head by kings and queens, and is often made of gold. A *crowned head* is a head wearing such a crown.

If you fly over the Nazca Desert along the southern coast of Peru, you will see huge drawings etched in the sand: a monkey, a spider, condors, flowers, triangles, rectangles, zigzags, spirals. Even human forms with crowned heads. And straight lines spreading out from a circle, like spokes from the hub of a wheel.

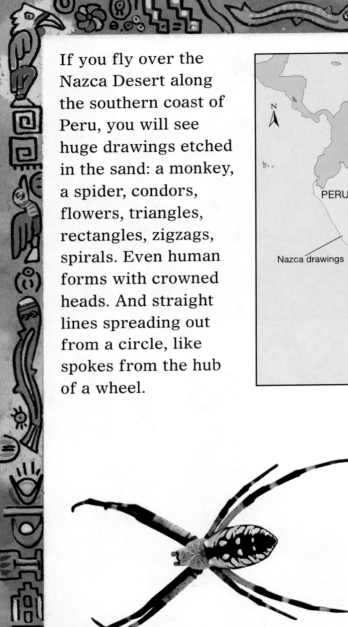

PERU

SOUTH AMERICA

Nazca drawings

The drawings seem endless. Some are more than six hundred feet from end to end, longer than two football fields. Some continue for miles, up hills and down valleys. In all, the markings cover 250 square miles of desert. Some drawings are so large that you can tell what they are only if you look at them from the air. But no one knows how they got there, or why.

Study Tip
Topic Sentences
The topic sentence states the main idea of a paragraph. The other sentences in the paragraph give details, or more information, about the main idea. The topic sentence can appear anywhere in a paragraph, but is often the first sentence. Look for the topic sentence as you read.

We do know they were made about two thousand years ago, by South American Indians called the Nazcas. The Nazca people lived in a green valley just below a huge stretch of desert called the *pampa*, meaning "flat place." The air around the pampa is hot and dry, and the pampa gets only about a half inch of rain each year. So the markings made long ago on its sandy, stony surface have not been worn away by the weather even after two thousand years.

When you look at the huge drawings, you can't help but wonder: Why would people make drawings that can be seen only from the air?

Strategy Tip
Predict
Why do you think the Nazcas' drawings were made to be seen from the air?

Many people have tried to answer this
question. Some think the drawings were a
way of communicating with traditional gods
and nature spirits. Others think the markings
were some sort of calendar that showed the
risings and settings of the sun, moon, and
stars—information important for Nazca
agriculture. Still others think the Nazcas must
have known how to fly. And some even think
the drawings were landing strips for visitors
from other planets.

To understand the Nazca drawings, scientists studied objects the Nazcas left behind. They found old pottery, textiles, and pieces of clothing made long ago by the Nazca people.

Some of these show pictures of flying or gliding gods. But did the Nazcas ever do more than just *think* about flying?

Strategy Tip
Draw Conclusions
Why do you think it was important for the International Explorers Society to use natural materials to make their balloon?

In 1975, researchers from the International Explorers Society did an experiment to find out if the Nazcas might have been able to fly in a hot-air balloon. Using natural materials and construction methods the Nazcas would have known about, they built a large balloon. They did get it up in the air, but not for long. Although the experiment showed that the Nazcas *could* have flown in a balloon, no evidence at all exists on the pampa that they actually tried to.

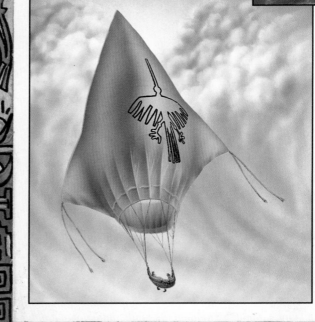

To find more clues about why the drawings were made, we can turn to history and anthropology. We know that Spain conquered Peru more than four hundred years ago—in 1532. The Spaniards destroyed much of the Peruvian way of life, except in remote regions of the Andes mountains. Today, descendants of the Peruvian natives who survived live in villages along the mountainsides. Farmers there have to hike thousands of feet each day to reach their fields. On their way, many of them perform religious ceremonies. Those ceremonies offer clues to the meaning of the Nazca lines.

Language Tip
Vocabulary
Anthropology is the scientific study of human beings, especially their customs, culture, and beliefs.

Strategy Tip
Reread
Turn back to pages 158 and 159 and reread the information there about the Spanish defeat of the Incas.

Language Tip
Vocabulary
Littered with means "thickly covered with."

Language Tip
Vocabulary
A *procession* is a kind of parade made on foot, sometimes as part of a religious ceremony.

When you look at the drawings from the ground, the lines look like pathways. Along the pathways are stone mounds, littered with scraps of broken pottery. The pathways resemble the mountain paths where today's farmers make their religious processions. The farmers leave offerings at stone mounds, which they call *wa'kas*, meaning shrines. The offerings include pieces of pottery, seashells, coca leaves, and food.

In these sacred ceremonies, farmers ask the mountain gods and animal spirits of the Andes to send them water. Since similar offerings are found on the lines and mounds of the pampa, it is likely that the ancient Nazcas had similar beliefs. And since the pampa is one of the driest deserts on earth, it makes sense that the Nazcas would worship gods that brought them water. Perhaps the drawings were meant to be viewed by the gods.

Today in Peru, native healers perform sacred healing ceremonies. They often call upon supernatural animals to help them. Many of the animals are the same as the ones that are drawn on the pampa. This, too, makes researchers think that the drawings were part of the Nazcas' most sacred traditions.

Language Tip
Vocabulary
Sacred means "holy."
Supernatural means "magical" or "larger-than-life."

Some people believe that the important thing about the drawings is that they show us a glimpse of a group of people who survived in a difficult climate by living in harmony with nature. The drawings seem to be part of a way of looking at nature, life, and spirit in a way that honored the connections among all things.

Perhaps we will never know the real meaning of the Nazca lines. But we do know that even though the Nazcas had none of our modern technology and few of the comforts of our modern society, they did extraordinary things. They made pottery and cloth with so much detail and color that it is believed to be some of the best ever made. They developed superior irrigation canals for watering their fields. And then, too, they left us those mysterious drawings in the sand, leaving us wondering still about the people who made them.

The Happy Wanderer

Words by Antonia Ridge

I love to go a-wandering, along the mountain track,
And as I go, I love to sing, my knapsack on my back.
Val-de ri Val-de ra Val-de ra Val-de ha ha ha ha ha ha
Val-de ri Val-de ra
My knapsack on my back.

I love to wander by the stream that dances in the sun,
So joyously it calls to me, "Come! Join my happy song!"
Val-de ri Val-de ra Val-de ra Val-de ha ha ha ha ha ha
Val-de ri Val-de ra
"Come! Join my happy song!"

Tell what you learned.

CHAPTER 9

1. What are some mysteries about the Inca?

2. Would you like to visit Machu Picchu? Why or why not?

3. What are the Nazca lines? What are some ideas about why people made the lines? What do you think the lines were for?

How Science Solves Mysteries

Tell what you know.

Can you solve these mysteries?

◀ The first photographs of the planet Mars showed straight lines like this. What caused the lines? People wondered whether there was life on Mars.

▲ Some Antarctic icebergs look green. Why?

▲ Some people have seen strange things flying in the sky. What could they be?

◄ People who lived near the Arctic Circle saw these strange lights in the sky. What could they be?

Talk About It

What unexplained mysteries do you know? Do you want to solve them? Why?

What makes the whales sing?

For many years, people have heard the strange sounds of whales singing. The whales' songs go on for a long time, sometimes for more than thirty minutes. They are so loud that people can hear them through the bottom of a wooden boat!

Scientists had many questions about the songs. Why do only a few kinds of whales sing? Why do the songs sound so different from other sounds whales make, such as clicks and squeaks? Why do different groups of whales sing different songs? Why are the songs so long?

You can take a special boat ▶ trip to watch whales.

Scientists followed whales for miles ▶
to make observations about them.

Scientists wanted to solve these mysteries. They began to collect **observations** about whales. Observations are things people see or notice. Scientists carefully wrote down where and when people heard whales singing. They also used special tools to record the songs.

Scientists then made **hypotheses,** informed guesses, based on their observations. They decided that whales use sounds to communicate. Scientists wondered if they sang to claim feeding waters and to keep other whales away. Did whales sing to woo, or attract, a mate? Did they sing to find one another in the ocean? Or were the whales just talking to each other?

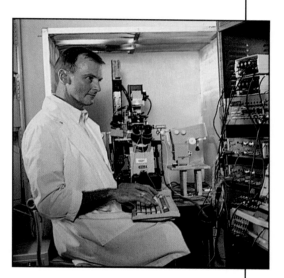

▲ Scientists study whales' songs with computers.

? Think About It

Based on the information in the text, what is your hypothesis about the whales' songs?

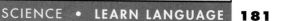

What did scientists find out about whales' songs?

The scientists tested their hypotheses by watching whales for a long time. They tried to find out which hypotheses might be **confirmed,** or found to be true. They also wanted to find out which hypotheses could be **disproved,** or found not to be true.

Scientists observed that all the whales in a group sang the same song. Since the songs did not change much, they could not mean different things, such as "Watch out!" or "Food is here." This seemed to disprove the hypothesis that the whales were talking.

▲ When humpback whales sing, they hang head down in the water.

Scientists confirmed that only male whales sing. Males sing during breeding season, when they look for partners. This made scientists think that male whales used their songs to impress females. It also made them think that the songs keep other males away. Scientists already knew that many male fish and animals compete with one another for females.

Scientists still don't know everything about whale songs. During breeding season, the songs slowly change to a new song. Males will start the next breeding season with the new song. But scientists don't know why. Scientists must make new hypotheses.

THE SONGS AND SOUNDS OF
THE HUMPBACK WHALE

Think About It

Only male whales sing. Does this help to confirm or disprove the idea that the songs are a way whales talk to each other?

Can you solve the mystery?

One day this road was flat. The next day
it was bumpy.

▲ The earth is made of layers of rock and soil. These
layers can be moved by water or earthquakes.

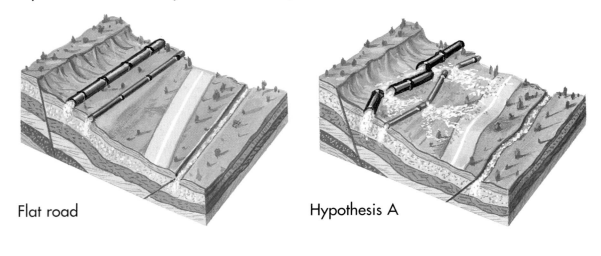

Flat road   Hypothesis A

People wanted to solve the mystery of what happened to the road. Here are some hypotheses:

Hypothesis A:

Big water pipes buried under the road broke. The water from the broken pipes washed away some of the dirt under the road.

Hypothesis B:

A heavy thunderstorm the night before caused a flood. Flood waters washed away the dirt under the road.

Hypothesis C:

An earthquake made the road bumpy.

Which of these hypotheses do you think is correct? Why? Can you think of another hypothesis for why the road became bumpy?

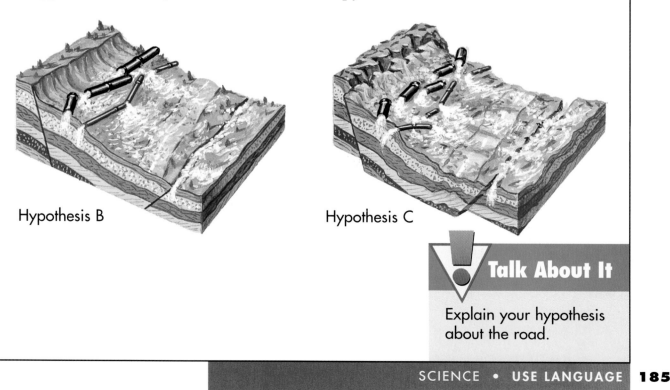

Hypothesis B

Hypothesis C

Talk About It

Explain your hypothesis about the road.

Mysteries

Solve the mystery of the black bag!

Puzzle 1

The bag has ten blocks in it. The blocks are red, white, and blue. Can you find out how many blocks of each color are inside? Use these clues.

Clues:

1. White blocks = red blocks.

2. There are more blue blocks than white blocks.

3. There is one more of the blue blocks than of the red blocks.

 Try It Out

Make your own mystery bag. Write clues so a friend can solve the mystery.

? same number of red and white blocks

? only 7

= 10

Puzzle 2

You have 10 tennis balls in your gym locker.

Some are orange, some are white, and some are green.

How many balls of each color are in your gym locker?

Clues:

1. There are three more white balls than green balls.

2. White balls + green balls = orange balls.

Puzzle 3

There are 20 muffins baking in the oven. The muffins are banana, raisin, and lemon. How many of each flavor are in the oven?

Clues:

1. There are more raisin muffins than banana muffins.

2. There is one more banana muffin than there are lemon muffins.

3. The number of lemon muffins + 4 = the number of raisin muffins.

Write About It

Make up other mystery puzzles like the ones on this page. Write them down and ask your friends to solve them.

The Loch Ness Monster

For hundreds of years, people have said they saw a monster in a cold lake in Scotland called Loch Ness. They said it looks like a big lizard or snake with flippers and a long neck. Some people think it is a giant seal or reptile. Others think it is a new and unknown animal. Many people think it really doesn't exist.

Scientists have tried to solve the mystery of the monster. They have used scientific knowledge to examine different ideas about the monster.

▲ Some people say they have taken photographs of the Loch Ness monster.

Some reports say the monster looks like a dolphin or a whale, but bigger. However, these animals are mammals. Mammals breathe air, and must come to the surface to breathe. So scientists say that if it were a mammal, many people would see it as it came up for air.

Some people say the monster might be a huge reptile trapped in the deep lake. But reptiles are cold-blooded. Scientists say that the lake is too cold for a reptile to live in.

Scientists used sonar and special cameras to explore beneath Loch Ness. They found no proof of a monster in Loch Ness. However, people still regularly report seeing the monster!

Hikers Report Seeing The Loch Ness Monster!

Dateline, Loch Ness, Scotland —
A man and a woman on an morning hike through the Scotland's

when I turned around and dark shape in the water," "I'm still not sure what it can take a guess."
Authorities believ

? Think About It

How could scientists prove once and for all whether there is a monster in Loch Ness?

Watching Gray Whales

by J. S. Baird

Their skin is gray-green.
They look like copper
    that is corroded.
Barnacles on them
    look like sharp
    rocks that are
    fixed to the
    sliding wall
    of a building
    under water.
They are of
    a different
    world, slow,
    watching you
    while you
    watch them.
They are patient.
They survive.

Tell what you learned.

1. What was your favorite mystery in this chapter? Why was it your favorite?

2. What hypotheses did scientists have about whales' songs? What information proves or disproves each hypothesis? Make a chart.

3. What other mystery in science have you read about? What would you do to solve the mystery?

Deserts

Word Bank

cold

dry

hot

sandy

sunny

thirsty

Tell what you know.

What is a desert?

What would it be like to walk in a desert?
What would you see? What would you feel?
What would you hear?

Talk About It

Have you ever visited a
desert? Where was it?
What was it like?

193

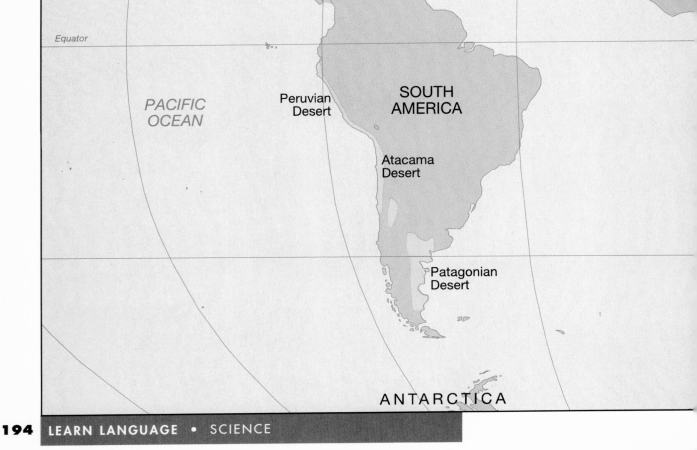

CHAPTER 11

Desert Life

NORTH
AMERICA

Great
Basin
Desert

What is a desert?

A desert is a place that gets less than 10 inches (25 centimeters) of **precipitation** in a year. Precipitation is rain or snow.

In some deserts, almost no rain falls at all. Other deserts may get all their rain for the year in one single day.

Equator

PACIFIC
OCEAN

Peruvian
Desert

SOUTH
AMERICA

Atacama
Desert

Patagonian
Desert

ANTARCTICA

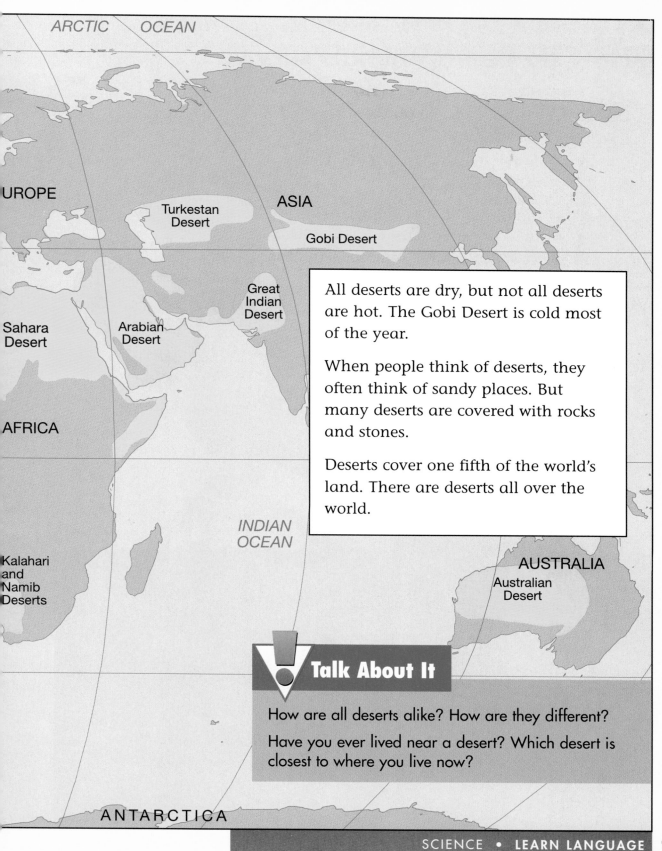

ARCTIC OCEAN

UROPE

ASIA

Turkestan
Desert

Gobi Desert

Great
Indian
Desert

Sahara
Desert

Arabian
Desert

AFRICA

All deserts are dry, but not all deserts are hot. The Gobi Desert is cold most of the year.

When people think of deserts, they often think of sandy places. But many deserts are covered with rocks and stones.

Deserts cover one fifth of the world's land. There are deserts all over the world.

INDIAN
OCEAN

Kalahari
and
Namib
Deserts

AUSTRALIA
Australian
Desert

Talk About It

How are all deserts alike? How are they different?

Have you ever lived near a desert? Which desert is closest to where you live now?

ANTARCTICA

How do desert animals survive?

Desert animals have special **adaptations** to help
them survive in hot, dry deserts. Adaptations
are special things animals have or do to
help them survive.

Some desert animals adapt by finding new
sources of water. The spiny lizard does not need
to drink water. It gets all the water it needs from
eating insects. Insect bodies contain enough
water for the lizard.

The gila woodpecker's long bill is an adaptation to help it get food. It uses this special bill to dig out insects in cactuses.

Other animals' adaptations help them keep cool. When animals' bodies get too hot, they lose water through their skin by **evaporation.**

The kit fox's large ears are an adaptation to help it keep cool. The fox loses extra body heat through its ears. Kit foxes also stay cool by living underground during the day, and only hunting for food at night.

Talk About It

How do adaptations help animals survive in the desert?

What helps a cactus survive in the desert?

Plants such as the cactus also have adaptations to life in the desert. If you touch a cactus, you will find that it has a waxy skin. Do this experiment to see how this skin helps the cactus survive.

Things You Need

3 paper towels   sheet of waxed paper

2 paper clips   1 plastic tray   spray bottle

Follow these steps.

1. Spray water on the paper towels. Make the towels damp, but not dripping wet.

2. Flatten out one of the paper towels. Place it on the tray.

3. Roll up the second paper towel. Place it on the tray.

4. Roll up the third paper towel. Then roll the waxed paper around it. Fasten the roll with a paper clip on each end. Then place the roll on the tray.

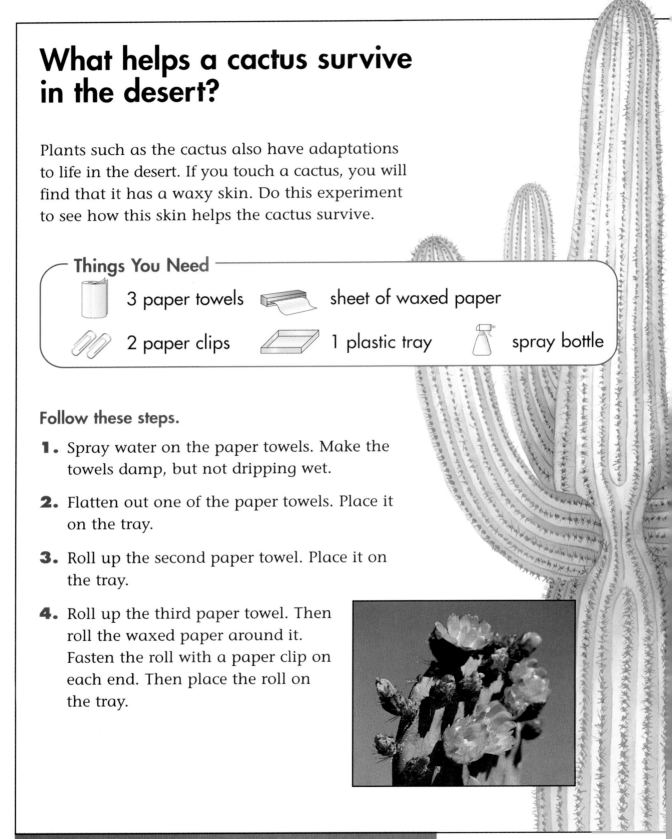

5. Put the tray in sunlight.

6. After a few hours, examine the towels. How does each feel?

7. Record the results.

		Paper towel: Dry, damp, or wet?
Flat		
Rolled up		
Rolled up with waxed paper		

My Record

Think About It

How does the cactus's waxy skin help it survive in the desert?

People in the Desert

There are few plants and little food in the dry desert. People need to adapt to live there.

Some people who live in the desert are **nomads.** They move from place to place.

Some nomads hunt wild animals for food. They eat insects and roots of desert plants. Insects and roots contain water. Other nomads raise goats and camels for meat and milk. These animals can survive with little water.

Nomads use tents for shelter. Living in tents helps nomads adapt to life in the desert. Nomads can put up and take down tents quickly when they move.

Tents can be adapted to different desert **temperatures.** Many deserts are hot during the day and cold at night. Nomads can fold the sides of the tents up to let wind flow in during the hot day. They can fold the sides of the tents down to hold in warm air at night.

Write About It

What things would you take with you to live in a nomad tent?

Jealous Goomble-Gubbon

by Lucy Baker

Strategy Tip
Setting
Look back at the map on pages 194 and 195 and find Australia. Locate the desert.

For thousands of years people have told stories about the world around them. Often these stories try to explain something that people do not really understand, like how the world began, or where light comes from. This tale is told by the aboriginal people of Australia.

Long ago in Australia was the Dream Time when everything was made. The land was made, with mountains, plains, and valleys full of all sorts of animals, birds, and plants. And the sea was made, full of whales, dolphins, and plants, but there were not yet any fish.

All the birds had been given wonderful and extraordinary voices: Crow croaked his rasping caw, Kookaburra laughed her hilarious chuckle, and the other birds sang in all their different voices. They sat singing in the trees and bushes all day long, because they were so happy.

Strategy Tip
Look for Sound Words
In this part of the story, many words tell about the sounds that birds make. A *caw* is the hard sound a crow makes. A *chuckle* is a small laugh.

Reader's Tip
Vocabulary
The kookaburra is a bird that lives in Australia. It makes a sound like a laugh.

When I say that they all had wonderful and extraordinary voices, I am forgetting Goomble-Gubbon, the turkey. Goomble-Gubbon could only make a low bubbling noise in his throat, which sounded like this: "goomble gubbon, goomble gubbon." All the other birds thought Goomble-Gubbon's voice was a great joke and they sang even more beautifully when he was around just to tease him.

Language Tip
Vocabulary
To tease someone is to make fun of him or her. About what thing did the other birds tease Goomble-Gubbon?

Of course, they didn't really mean to be cruel. They were all so happy themselves that they did not realize how much they were hurting poor Goomble-Gubbon's feelings. They were very fond of him, in spite of his bad-tempered ways.

Strategy Tip
Understand Conflict
Conflict in a story is a problem a character has with someone or something. What is the conflict between Goomble-Gubbon and the other birds?

Goomble-Gubbon did not find his voice funny. He thought it was terrible and he was very jealous of all the other birds' voices. He tried everything he could to improve his voice, but nothing was any use. If only the other birds' voices were not so wonderful and extraordinary, his voice would not seem so terrible, he thought.

One day was worse than ever before. The other birds had been laughing at Goomble-Gubbon all morning and he was tired of it. So he went off to visit his friend Lizard. Lizard never laughed at his voice. The two of them sat talking and telling stories until the sun began to set. Just then, Kookaburra flew into the branches of a nearby tree and began to laugh.

Strategy Tip
Understand Personification
When animals talk and act like people, we call that *personification*. Can you think of other stories where personification is used?

Language Tip
Idiom
*To be fed up is to be
angry about something
and be very tired of it.*

Now, Kookaburra could not help laughing. She laughed at everything, even at things that were not at all funny, and Goomble-Gubbon should have known this really. But he was fed up with being teased by all the other birds, and so he thought that Kookaburra had flown over and perched on that very branch just to laugh at him.

"What do you think you're laughing at?" he snapped angrily.

Kookaburra looked most surprised and flew off to tell the other birds about Goomble-Gubbon's strange behavior.

Strategy Tip
Understand Vocabulary
Use the other words in the sentence to guess the meaning of *snapped*.

Language Tip
Idiom
To make up your mind is to decide to do something.

Language Tip
Idiom
To set something alight means to start a fire.

Meanwhile Goomble-Gubbon made up his mind to put a stop to the other birds' teasing once and for all. He waited until it was dark and all the birds were asleep in the trees. Then, very quietly, he went to the magic burning tree. This was a tree where men took their firesticks to fetch fire for food, warmth, and light for their camps. Goomble-Gubbon picked up a stick from the ground and lit it from the tree. Then he crept around to all the trees and bushes where the birds were sleeping and set the bottom branches alight.

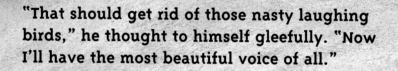

Study Tip
Research Skills
To learn more about deserts, go to the library. Look up *desert* in the card or computer catalog. Report what you find out.

"That should get rid of those nasty laughing birds," he thought to himself gleefully. "Now I'll have the most beautiful voice of all."

However, Kookaburra was not asleep. She heard Goomble-Gubbon creeping around beneath the trees and woke the other birds to warn them.

Language Tip
Vocabulary
A *swarm* is a very large group.

A great swarm of birds rose up from the trees, screeching and crying. The birds who could fly fast flew away as quickly as they could to far-off places where there was no fire. Those who could not fly fast enough to get away from the flames flew into the sea to cool off. As they entered the water, their wings turned into fins and their feathers became scales. At last there were fish in the sea!

Goomble-Gubbon was furious that his plan had not worked. He waved the firestick wildly, but only managed to singe his own feathers a nasty smoky color and burn his head bright red too. He threw the firestick far out into the bush.

The fire in the trees went on burning until the land in the center of Australia was quite barren and dry. And that is how the desert came to be in the center of Australia. All because of jealous Goomble-Gubbon.

Strategy Tip
Understand Vocabulary
Use the other words in the sentence to guess the meaning of singe.

Strategy Tip
Resolution
A story's resolution is how the conflict in the story is solved at the end. What is the resolution of Goomble-Gubbon's conflict with the other birds?

The Desert

by Malvina Reynolds

I sing of the desert,
The bushes are brave,
On the hot sandy plain
They root and survive
Without sprinkler or rain.

I sing of the desert,
The nights are so clear,
The air is so still,
You can reach for a star
Whenever you will.

I sing of the desert,
It's ample and wide,
And that's where I'll stay,
And that's where I'll bide,
And that's where I'll hide
Till the tide of the cities passes away.

Tell what you learned.

1. What makes a place a desert?

2. Tell how two desert animals have adapted to life in the desert.

3. Explain two ways people have adapted to life in the desert.

4. Can you think of another way Goomble-Gubbon might have solved his problem?

CHAPTER 12

Water in the Desert

Tell what you know.

Where could you find water in a desert? What happens in a desert after a rainfall?

Word Bank

canyon

flower

lightning

thunderstorm

well

Talk About It

How do people use water? How do you use water every day?

What happens in a desert after it rains?

Rain does not come often in a desert. Rainstorms come suddenly, and usually last a short time.

After a rainstorm, there is much activity in the desert. Animals and plants use the water from the rain quickly, before it runs off or evaporates.

After a rain, the spadefoot toad comes out of its home under the ground. It lays its eggs in pools of water made by the rain. It eats a meal of insects. Then it returns underground. It doesn't eat again until the next time it rains.

After a rain, tiny seeds grow into flowers. These flowers must grow quickly and make new seeds. The next time it rains, these new seeds will grow into flowers.

After a rain, the saguaro cactus quickly soaks up water. The roots carry water to the stem. The stem fills up with water. The stem gets thicker in size. The cactus stores enough water to last until the next rain.

before rain

after rain

Write About It

How do desert plants and animals adapt to use the sudden, heavy rain?

What is an oasis?

An **oasis** is an area in a desert where fresh water is close to the surface of the ground. Because of this water, an oasis has more plants and animals than other parts of the desert.

Oases allow people in the desert to do many things. Nomads travel from one oasis to another to find shade, food, rest, and water for themselves and their animals.

Some oases are very large. People live and build homes at larger oases. Some oases are so big that people can farm on them. Some are so big that people can build cities on them.

Riyadh, the capital of Saudi Arabia, is a large oasis. More than one million people live in Riyadh. The oasis supplies the city with water.

Oasis farmers near Riyadh can grow many different fruits and vegetables. They grow dates, olives, and melons. They sell them at the markets in Riyadh.

Word Bank

lake

reservoir

river

well

Talk About It

How does your town or city get water? Where is the water supply? Are there farmers near where you live? How do they get water?

How do people affect the water in the desert?

The water at oases is **ground water.** This is water that collects between layers of rock far below the surface. Ground water is pumped to the surface for people to use.

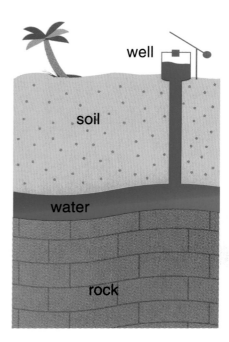

However, many sources of ground water in desert areas are drying up through overuse. When ground water dries up, water holes disappear. Desert plants and animals no longer have enough water to survive.

Many farmers in the dry areas in the western United States use ground water. They pump up the ground water and use it to **irrigate** their crops.

Some desert farmers irrigate their fields by covering them with water. These farmers use a lot of water.

But other desert farmers irrigate their fields by sprinkling. These farmers use less water. They **conserve** water.

Now many people want to conserve water. For example, a grass lawn needs a lot of watering to keep it green. Many people in dry areas want to conserve water. They make their gardens out of desert plants and rocks.

Grass lawn:
50 gallons a week

Desert lawn:
5 gallons a week

Think About It

How can you persuade other people that it is important to conserve water? What reasons can you give?

How much water do you use?

Even if you do not live in a desert, you can help conserve water. Look at the chart to see how much water people use for daily activities. How much water do you use each day? Think of ways you might cut down the amount of water you use.

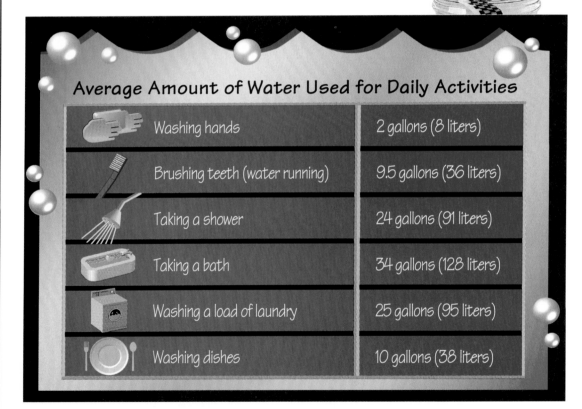

Average Amount of Water Used for Daily Activities	
Washing hands	2 gallons (8 liters)
Brushing teeth (water running)	9.5 gallons (36 liters)
Taking a shower	24 gallons (91 liters)
Taking a bath	34 gallons (128 liters)
Washing a load of laundry	25 gallons (95 liters)
Washing dishes	10 gallons (38 liters)

Try It Out

You can find out how much water you use when you brush your teeth. Place a bowl under the faucet while you brush your teeth. The sink will catch the water you use. Then use a measuring cup to find the amount of water in the bowl.

Now try brushing your teeth with the water off. Turn it on only to rinse your toothbrush. Catch the water in the bowl as you did before. Measure. How much water did you save by turning off the faucet?

Write About It

How much water do you use in a day? How much water do you use in a week? Use the chart to help you add and multiply to get the totals.

How much water will you save in a week if you brush your teeth without running the water? Multiply the amount of water you saved by seven.

Can you think of any other ways you can conserve water? Try to guess how much water you might save.

Southwest News

Our Opinion: Not Enough Water

People in cities say that farmers use too much water to irrigate their crops. Farmers answer that they are growing food people need. They say that people in cities waste too much water in their homes.

Environmentalists say that animals in our area need water.

CONNECT LANGUAGE • SCIENCE/READING

When farmers and city people use too much water, the water animals need to survive starts to dry up.

All of us need to stop fighting and start conserving water. Let's work together to think of new solutions to the problem of not enough water in our area.

We need to study all possible solutions. Some people have had the idea of bringing icebergs from the South Pole. The icebergs would melt and provide fresh water to cities. This may sound crazy, but who knows? Maybe it will work.

Let's listen to new ideas about how to solve the problem.

Write About It

Can you think of other solutions to the problem of not enough water in dry areas? Draw a picture of your solution. Write a caption for your picture.

Cool Water

Words and music by Bob Nolan

All day I've faced a barren waste without the
taste of water.
Cool water.
Old Dan and I with throats burnt dry and souls
that cry for water.
Cool, clear water.

The nights are cool, and I'm a fool, each star's a
pool of water.
Cool water.
But with the dawn I'll wake and yawn and carry
on to water.
Cool, clear water.

? Think About It

What do you think has
happened to the people
in this song? What do
you think will happen
to them?

Tell what you learned.

1. Think over the unit. How do animals, plants, and people adapt to life in the desert? Make a list of adaptations.

Which adaptations help in finding and keeping water? Which adaptations help in staying cool? Which adaptation do you think is the most interesting or unusual?

2. How can people help to conserve water?

3. Make a poster to help make people think about a way to conserve water.

Writer's Workshop

Follow these steps to be a good writer.

① Prewriting

Choose a topic.
List your ideas about the topic.
Ask friends for ideas.
Look in books for ideas.

family
friends
my neighborhood
celebrations and parties
school
sports
hobbies and things I like to do
places I have visited

Decide what you want to write.
Do you want to write a story?
Do you want to explain something?
Do you want to describe something?
Do you want to tell how you feel?

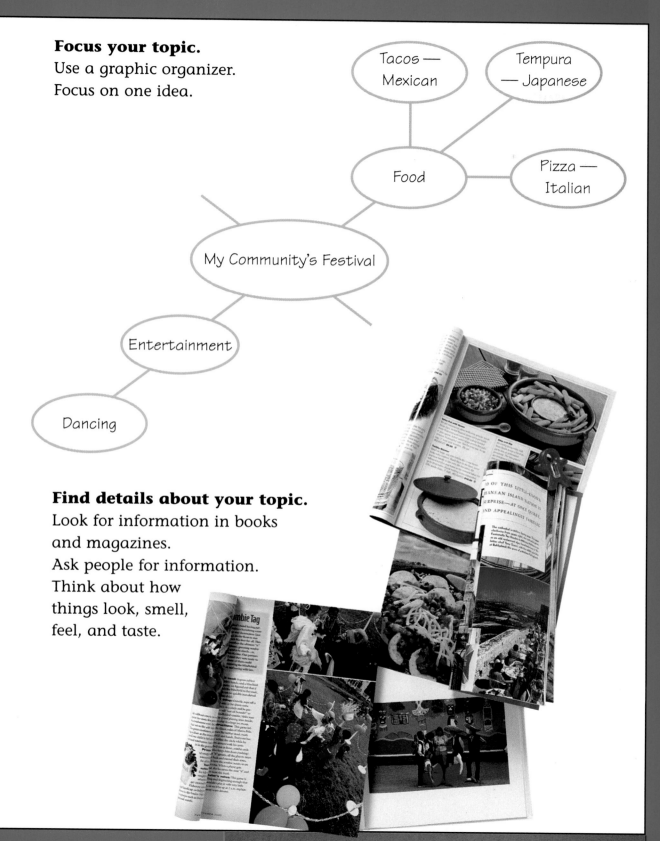

Focus your topic.

Use a graphic organizer.
Focus on one idea.

Tacos — Mexican

Tempura — Japanese

Food

Pizza — Italian

My Community's Festival

Entertainment

Dancing

Find details about your topic.

Look for information in books
and magazines.
Ask people for information.
Think about how
things look, smell,
feel, and taste.

② Drafting

Get what you need.
Get paper and pencils.
Get your graphic organizer and list of ideas.
Sit in a comfortable place.

Set a goal.
How much will you write now?

Read your notes.
What do you want
to say first?

Keep writing.
Write down all
your ideas.
Don't worry about
spelling and
punctuation now.

My Community's Festival

Last sumer my community had a big festival.
Restaurants in the community sold food at
small stands. We ate pizza from a Italian
restaurant and tacos from a Mexican
restaurant. I really liked the fried vegetables
called tempura from a japanese restaurant.

Dancers did dances from Ireland and Polish on a
stage they wore beautiful costumes from their
countries. After it gets dark, we watch fireworks.

❸ Revising

Read what you wrote. Ask yourself:
Does my story have a beginning, a middle, and an end?
Is my information correct?
What parts should I keep?
What parts should I leave out?

I think I need a better ending.

Talk with someone.
Show your writing to a friend or your teacher.
Do your readers understand your writing?

Who are the "we" in your story?

4 Proofreading

Check your spelling.
Look in a dictionary or ask for help.

Look for capital letters.

Look for correct punctuation.

Make a new copy.

☰ **Make a capital.**
╱ **Make a small letter.**
∧ **Add something.**
ℓ **Take out something.**
⊙ **Add a period.**
¶ **Make a new paragraph.**

My Community's Festival

Last sumer my community had a big festival.
I went to the festival with friends from my
school. Restaurants in the community sold food
at small stands. We ate pizza from a Italian
restaurant and tacos from a Mexican
restaurant. I really liked the fried vegetables
called tempura from a japanese restaurant.
Dancers did folk dances from Ireland and
Poland Polish on a stage they wore beautiful costumes
from their countries. After it gets dark, we
watch fireworks. I want to go to the festival
again next summer so I can taste more foods.
I can't wait!

⑤ Presenting

Share your writing.
Read it aloud to your family or classmates.
Make a book. Lend the book to your family
or classmates.

My Community's Festival

Last summer my community had a big festival.
I went to the festival with friends from my school.
Restaurants in the community sold food at small
stands. We ate pizza from an Italian restaurant
and tacos from a Mexican restaurant. I really
liked the fried vegetables called tempura from
a Japanese restaurant.

Dancers did folk dances from Ireland and
Poland on a stage. They wore beautiful costumes
from their countries. After it got dark, we
watched fireworks.

I want to go to the festival again next summer
so I can taste more foods. I can't wait!

What a Good Writer Can Do

- I plan before I write.

- I can write about things I know. I can write about my family, my school, and myself.

- I can write stories with a beginning, a middle, and an end.

- I can ask others to read my work.

- I can write in complete sentences.

- I can put periods at the end of sentences.

- I can make my handwriting easy to read.